Fortran Programming
with
Applications to Engineering

Jack B. Evett
University of North Carolina at Charlotte

Richard P. Pinckney
Lander College

Engineering Press, Inc.   San Jose, California 95103

Library of Congress Cataloging in Publication Data

Evett, Jack B
    Fortran programming with applications to engineering.
    Includes index.
    1. FORTRAN (Computer program language)
2. Engineering--Data processing. I. Pinckney,
Richard P.,   date   joint author. II. Title.
QA76.73.F25E93   001.64'24   80-22695
ISBN   0-910554-32-3

Printed in the United States of America

Engineering Press, Inc.   P.O. Box 1   San Jose, California 95103

To Linda, Susan, Scott, Sarah, and Sallie Evett
    and
    Susan, Matthew, Joy, and Ryan Pinckney

Contents

1 **Introduction to Computers and to Communicating with Computers** 1
  1-1 Organization of Computers 1
  1-2 The Programming of Computers 7
  1-3 The General Problem-Solving Process 9
  1-4 Flowcharting 10
  1-5 Methods of Communicating with the Processor 14

2 **Basic Concepts and Features of Fortran** 17
  2-1 Two Kinds of Numbers 17
  2-2 Constants and Variables 18
  2-3 Fortran Operations 19
  2-4 Fortran Expressions 19
  2-5 Arithmetic Assignment Statements 22
  2-6 Built-in Functions 23
  2-7 Problems 25

3 **Input/Output** 29
  3-1 Output Statements 29
  3-2 FORMAT Statements 31
  3-3 Data Input 41
  3-4 Free Format Input/Output 48
  3-5 Input/Output with Terminals 50
  3-6 Summary 51
  3-7 Problems 51

4 **The Fortran Program** 55
  4-1 Introduction 55
  4-2 Coding Requirements 55
  4-3 Program Development 57
  4-4 Example Programs 59
  4-5 "Debugging" the Program 65
  4-6 Problems 66

5 **Program Control** 69
  5-1 Introduction 69
  5-2 The GO TO Statement 69
  5-3 IF Statements 73
  5-4 Block-IF 82
  5-5 Problems 88

6 DO Loops and Subscripted Variables 91
  6-1 Introduction 91
  6-2 DO Loops 91
  6-3 Single Subscripted Variables 95
  6-4 Double Subscripted Variables 102
  6-5 Implied DO Loops....................................109
  6-6 Problems 113
7 The Statement Function and Subprograms 117
  7-1 Introduction 117
  7-2 The Statement Function..............................118
  7-3 The Function Subprogram 120
  7-4 The Subroutine Subprogram.........................125
  7-5 General Remarks and Warnings 131
  7-6 Problems 132
8 Applications 137
  8-1 Print Plotting 137
  8-2 Trial and Error 142
  8-3 Iterative Solutions...................................146
  8-4 Matrix Manipulations 151
  8-5 Statistical Analyses 158
  8-6 Conclusion 164
  8-7 Problems 166
9 Advanced Fortran IV Topics...........................169
  9-1 REAL and INTEGER Statements 169
  9-2 The IMPLICIT Statement 170
  9-3 The DOUBLE PRECISION Statement 171
  9-4 The COMPLEX Statement 173
  9-5 The LOGICAL Statement 175
  9-6 The COMMON Statement..........................178
  9-7 The EQUIVALENCE Statement 181
  9-8 The ENTRY Statement.............................183
  9-9 Adjustable Arrays....................................187
  9-10 A Comment 188
  9-11 Problems...188
10 Closure 191
  10-1 Fortran Recap/Results Achieved 191
  10-2 Implementation 192
  10-3 Additional Uses of Fortran 193
  10-4 The Future Utilization of Programming...........193
  10-5 One Last Opinion 194

Appendices
  A Fortran Built-in Functions............................ 197
  B Groups of Numbers for Data Input Assignment
      in Problems 201
  C Fortran Statements Using Fortran Key Words 203
Index 207

Fully Illustrated
Example Problems

Area by Coordinate Method 100
Area of Rectangular Lot.................................59
Average Velocity of Water Flow 64
Borrow Pit Volume Calculation 102
Determination of Two Legs and
    Included Angle of a Triangle 127
Linear Regression Line 159
Matrix Manipulations 151
Plotting 137
Reactions for Simple and Cantilever Beams 84
Roots of an Equation.................................... 146

Preface

With little doubt the major question on the mind of the person reading this preface for the first time is: "Why another book on Fortran?". There are four main reasons, and we would like to elaborate on these.

First, and foremost, we believe this book is written in easy-to-read, easy-to-understand, everyday language. We know other authors will make the same claim about their books, and we would certainly not try to disclaim those. Nevertheless, we do believe our book meets this criterion very favorably. We have used a set of notes, from which this book was derived, for a number of years in teaching freshman engineering students, and the results have been very successful. More importantly perhaps, we have had several occasions where individuals, who have been studying Fortran using another book and having trouble, have come upon a copy of our notes and have benefited significantly from them. (At least, that's what they told us.) We will leave it up to the reader and the student to decide whether or not this is true, but we do hope you will give our book one try.

Second, we believe the order in which the material is presented is good for getting the student to writing programs as soon as possible. We cover basic concepts initially, followed by Input/Output (I/O). With a knowledge of basic concepts (including arithmetic assignment statements) and I/O, a number of simple programs are possible, such as defining (using arithmetic assignments statements) one or more data, plugging them into a formula, and writing out the answer(s). Having covered this, we then tell our students that it would generally be a waste of time to go to the trouble of writing a program, punching it, and running it just to solve one equation for one set of data. But, one of the benefits of using the computer is its ability to do repetitive computations. Thus if control statements are covered next, the simple program utilizing concepts and I/O can be expanded to increment one of the input parameters and compute and write out another answer. Of course, the program can be made to increment, compute, and write out 100, 1000, or any number of answers. The student can now begin to see the value of using the computer, as one simple program will now do hundreds or thousands of computations quickly and accurately. We then point out that, while this type of program is useful for many purposes, it is somewhat limited by the fact that only one variable was allowed to change and then always by the same increment. Wouldn't it be nice to be able to vary all the input parameters, but not necessarily by the same increment? This can, of course, be done by placing a read statement inside a "loop" so that each time through the loop, new values of *all* the input parameters can be read. We then cover the DO loop as a short-cut method for setting up the loop for the previous program. Next to be covered is the subscripted variable, which is introduced as a convenient means of handling large quantities of data — particularly when data must be read and stored, such as in sorting. Finally, the statement function and subprograms are covered as a means of doing the same computation(s) at several different locations in a program without having to repeat the programming steps each time.

Third, we have included a number of problems at the end of most chapters. Also, we have tried to make the problems interesting and practical whenever possible, rather than just exercises. There are several problems of the type "what would the computer write out?". These consist of a program or program segment, which the student must follow through step by step — just as the computer would — and determine what the computer would write out when the write statement is encountered. We believe this is a very effective teaching technique, as going through an already written program step by step helps the student understand programming logic. It also assists the student in "debugging" his or her program. We have also included a number of simple problems, such as short answer questions, find the error in these Fortran statements, etc. All in all, we believe the problems in this book constitute one of its major assets. Additionally, Appendix B contains lists of numbers to be assigned by the instructor. This will simplify the process of providing data.

Fourth, we have included from time to time what we would call programming "tips." After helping students "debug" programs for many years, we believe we must have seen most of the mistakes that can be made in programming. Often students overlook simple errors while searching for more serious ones. Students assume errors are sophisticated errors in logic; whereas frequently the error is something simple like starting a statement in column 6 (continuation column) or mispunching a variable name at one point so that it is no longer the same variable that appears elsewhere in the program. The latter error is very subtle and difficult to spot by the untrained eye. We certainly do not claim to be able to eliminate these, but we do believe the "tips" included throughout the text will help students minimize such errors and will also help students "debug" their programs. Also noteworthy, we believe, is the emphasis on both flow charts and comment cards. For every example problem, beginning with the easiest, we have included a flow chart and comment cards.

This book is aimed toward engineering students who are beginning their study of Fortran programming. However, we really believe it would be a good book for anyone wishing to learn Fortran or "brush up" on it. The basic discussion of Fortran is general and certainly requires no knowledge of engineering; and the problems, although of an engineering nature, are generally self-explanatory and also require no knowledge of engineering. Additionally, the text is written in such a manner that it can be used for independent study or as a text in a lecture course. For these reasons, we hope the reader will find this a very useful as well as useable book. We would be happy to receive any comments or suggestions.

Finally, we wish to express publicly our sincere appreciation to our colleagues and friends, Carlos G. Bell and Frank S. Preston, who read the manuscript and offered many helpful suggestions, and to Renda Gwaltney, who typed the manuscript.

Jack B. Evett

Richard P. Pinckney

Fortran Programming

with

Applications to Engineering

1
Introduction to Computers and to Communicating with Computers

It took more than ten years following the development of the first computers to develop the now universally-accepted idea of computer programming languages. Why such a delay? To answer this question requires some understanding of the operation of any digital computer. The evolution of programming languages depended upon the advancement of computer technology and man's eagerness to avoid unusual amounts of programming effort.

This chapter is devoted to presenting a description of the organization of digital computers and to explaining the manner in which a person can utilize these computers. The organization of computers of various manufacturers may differ in characteristics of specific components, but most will each have certain components performing similar functions. The efficient use of the computer is dependent on a complete, well-defined communication system between the person using the computer and the computer itself. To employ the computer this person must first clearly understand the problem with which he or she is involved. This is because the computer must receive well-defined messages instructing it on what must be done so that meaningful results may be returned.

1-1 ORGANIZATION OF COMPUTERS

Examination of the organization of a general-purpose computer can give valuable insight into the development of the art of communicating with the computer. Every computer must have some form of human-generated instructions in order to function correctly. These instructions are communicated to the computer as a whole through an input unit. The form that the input takes can vary, but the beginning user will usually input each problem either through card readers or through an on-line terminal (Figures 1-1 and 1-2 present two types of on-line terminals used for input and output).

Once the computer has received the set of human-generated instructions (that it must have to complete its assigned task of problem-solving), the computer will store these instructions in its memory unit. Thus two additional units are needed to execute these steps — a memory and a controller for routing information to and from memory. The controller's operation is governed by a separate computer program which has been designed by the computer manufacturer. The controller decides when to receive input, where to store it, and also acts as the supervisor for all the actions inside the computer.

Each instruction stored by the controller is placed in a separate location in a part of the memory called a storage register. The contents of a storage register may be examined, changed, or recalled by the controller whenever necessary. Other information, such as various sets of data, may be stored in the memory unit for the execution of particular sets of instructions.

Various types of memory devices are available. The frequency of access needed by the controller helps determine the type of memory device that should be used for storing data. For example, data referenced frequently by more-active parts of the computer might be stored on a fast-access, expensive flip-flop memory device. Data referenced only rarely might be stored on a slower and less-expensive device such as a magnetic drum.

The more sophisticated the controller unit, the more work the entire computer is capable of performing. Of course, the sophistication of the controller is influenced both by the quality of the electronic components of the computer and by the special instructions prepared for the controller.

The degree of sophistication of a controller is closely related to how fast "messages" may be transmitted between the controller and the four other major units. Messages (information) may be transmitted easily and quickly within a computer in the form of electrical codes. Groups of wires can be taken together to actually represent ideas through combinations of on (current present) and off (current not present) states in the groups of wires. In the same

Figure 1-1   A cathode ray tube terminal for remote computer access (The IBM 3278 terminal - courtesy of IBM Corp.)

Figure 1-2 A printing terminal for remote computer access (The IBM 3774 terminal - courtesy of IBM Corp.)

way groups of dots and dashes can represent letters of the alphabet in Morse code, the presence or absence of electrical currents in the groups of wires can mean certain instructions to and from the controller.

Two other basic components of a computer are involved in the execution of a set of instructions. The arithmetic unit performs necessary calculations, and the output unit makes a response to the user.

Through its binary circuitry, the arithmetic unit performs logical operations including the basic functions of addition, subtraction, multiplication, and division. The controller indicates which of the operations is to be performed and supplies the numbers to be used by the arithmetic unit.

Output may be chosen to come in various ways: punched cards, teletype-terminal display, cathode-ray tube (CRT) terminal display, high-speed printers onto paper, graphical output, or into auxiliary memory units. The most common types of output units for users from science and engineering are printed paper and terminal display. Again, the controller directs output to the correct output device as specified by the user.

Thus the five major components of any general-purpose computer are the input unit, the memory unit, the arithmetic unit, the output unit, and the controller. Figure 1-3 below shows these five units and paths of interaction that are possible. Although all

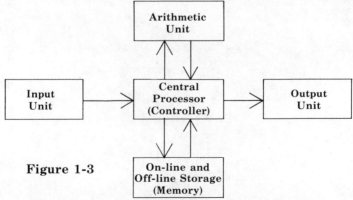

Figure 1-3

Relationship of the Components of a General-Purpose Computer

of the five component units of the general-purpose computer are important, by far the dominant unit is the controller.

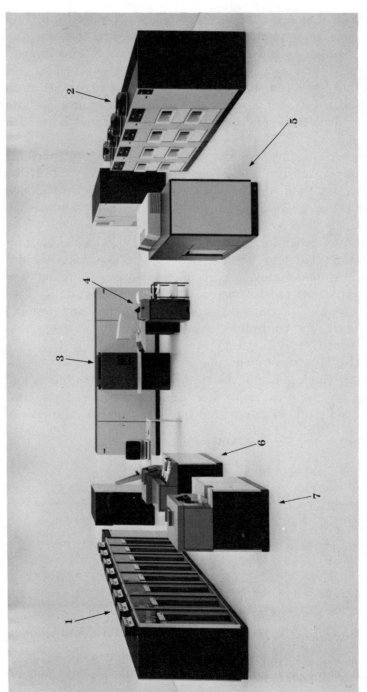

Figure 1-4.   A large-scale computer system. The major units of this, the IBM 370/158 system, are: 1) Magnetic tape drives; 2) disk drives; 3) the central processing unit (CPU); 4) the operator's terminal (a CRT type with auxiliary printer); 5) a high-speed line printer; 6) a punched-card reader; 7) an output card punch. (Courtesy of IBM Corp.)

Figure 1-4 displays a modern large-scale computer system. User-directed input can come from units numbered 1, 2, and 6. The separate memory units are denoted as 1 and 2. The controller and arithmetic unit are pictured as number 3. Numbers 5 and 7 mark two output units. The unit numbered 4 is the operator's console for system monitoring.

1-2 THE PROGRAMMING OF COMPUTERS

The brief description presented in the last section of the communication of information between the major components of a general-purpose computer refers to the use of a special language known as machine language. Since the transmission of messages is so very fast and the number of possible messages must be great for a general-purpose computer, the components of the *machine* (the computer itself) are the only entities that can derive any great meaning or use from communicating via these groups of electrical signals; thus, the name *machine* language. Man of course created the language for the machine, but man can not react to the signals fast enough to use that same language for communication with a computer. On the other hand, if the machine were to use only a language for internal communication that was easily interpreted by humans, less time would be saved by employing a computer.

To summarize, the sophisticated communication system of a computer must be capable of very rapid internal operation; however, this communication system must not also demand tedious, time-consuming programming effort by people using the computer. Thus a necessary link was developed for individuals who did not want to communicate in machine language with a computer. This link in the overall communication system was an "interpreter" between a user not "speaking" machine language and the computer's controller, which only communicates in machine language. This link is referred to as a compiler or *processor*.

A processor is a programmed set of instructions that can translate instructions entered by a user into machine language. The instructions entered by a user are often in words easily understood by the person using the computer. The machine language translation of each of these words may involve many controller instructions. By allowing the computer to perform the translation of user instructions, much user time is saved because the computer is able to translate user-defined operations much faster than the user could.

The translated set of user instructions is collectively referred to as the "object" code of user instructions. The object code is maintained until the computer actually performs the tasks indicated by the user instructions. This performance is referred to as the "execution" of the program.

A compiler is a processor that has been constructed for a specific set of key words. The compiler is usually a vast set of complex instructions, which allows much flexibility by the user. One of the most widely used compilers is the Fortran compiler (in many different forms). Fortran's popularity has been achieved because of: (1) its broad range of applications; (2) the close correspondence of statements in Fortran to related arithmetic concepts; and (3) Fortran has established standards. This makes Fortran coding easily formulated and interpreted.

To give a more concise representation of the ideas in Sec. 1-2, Fig. 1-5 illustrates, for a simple Fortran program, the following:
   a) the listing of the Fortran statements as submitted through punched cards or a teletype terminal console;
   b) the Fortran-generated "macro" coding which is an assembly language translation of the program;
   c) a portion of the Fortran-generated "octal" coding which is a translation of the macro coding.

One last step (which is not illustrated and may actually be considered several steps) is a translation to the "binary" coding of the octal coding.

As one may observe, each translation involves more coding. The objective of the translations from the "high" level language Fortran to the lowest level of the binary coding is again to permit representation of ideas or data using the presence or absence of electrical currents (a "binary" indicator).

The exact purpose of the Fortran statements illustrated may not be clear to the reader at this point; however, the authors' intent is to remove some of the mystery surrounding the handling of user input to a computer. Note in Fig. 1-5 the compactness of the Fortran listing. The macro and octal codings tend to greatly expand the listing. The binary coding would border on voluminous. Being able to avoid working with such great quantities of data does relieve a programmer of much responsibility.

```
00001              INTEGER I,J                          000006000002
00002              DO 10 I=1,5                          000000000000
00003              J=J+I                                000343324245
00004      10      CONTINUE                             0200L0000000
00005              WRITE(6,100)J
00006     100      FORMAT(' THE SUM IS:',I3)            000001000002
00007              STOP                                 200000000000
00008              END                                  000000000010
                                                        777773000001
```

a) The listing of a Fortran program

```
                                                        000003000002
                                                        200000000000
                                                        400000400000
                                                        000011000000

                                                        000001000005
LINE   LOC    LABEL   GENERATED CODE                    200000000000
                                                        000000000004
       0              JFCL   0,0                        241164052220
       1              JSP    16,RESET.                  425012352632
       2                     0,0                        202232335116
2      3              MOVE   2,[777773000001]           262226324400
3      4      2M:
                      MOVEI  3,0(2)                      000001000022
       5              ADDM   3,J                         200424000100
4      6      10P:                                       000000400000
                      AOBJN  2,2M                        255000000000
5      7              MOVEI  16,3M                       265700000000
       10             PUSHJ  17,OUT.                     000000000000
       11             MOVEI  16,4M                       200100000010
       12             PUSHJ  17,IOLST.                   201142000000
7      13             MOVEI  16,1M                       272140000001
       14             PUSHJ  17,STOP.                    253100400004
8      15             MOVEI  16,1M                       201700000000
       16             PUSHJ  17,EXIT.                    260740000000
                                                        201700000000
```

b) The Fortran-generated "macro" coding of the listing in (a) above.

```
                                                        260740000000
                                                        201700000000
                                                        260740000000
                                                        201700400013
                                                        260740000000
                                                        000000000000
                                                        000000000000

                                                        000001000012
```

Figure 1-5. Computer Translation of a Fortran program (on a DEC-10 computer).

```
                                                        200101000000
                                                        000000400021
                                                        777773000000
                                                        000000000005
                                                        000000000000
                                                        000000000000
                                                        000340000004
                                                        000000000004
c) The Fortran-generated                                000000000000
    "octal" listing of (b)                              001100000001
                                                        004000000000
```

1-3 THE GENERAL PROBLEM-SOLVING PROCESS

Before any problem can be effectively communicated to a computer via a programming language like Fortran, the problem solver usually progresses through several stages, which are collectively referred to as the general problem solving process. The purpose of the stages is to insure a well organized approach to solving a problem. Frequently an attempt is made to solve a problem without studying the situation carefully. As a result, often the actual problem may not be solved or may be incorrectly "solved".

ghht"

The following is a listing of some of the stages in the general problem solving process using a computer solution approach:

1) Problem exists and is observed.
2) A person is assigned to solve the problem.
3) The problem is studied.
4) Data are gathered.
5) A model is made for the problem.
6) If useful, the logic of the model is programmed for computer manipulation. This includes flowcharting the logic of the model to construct more easily a correct computer program.
7) The model is used to reproduce an occurrence(s) of the observed condition(s).
8) If the model does satisfactorily reproduce the observed problem(s), then tests may be conducted using the model to determine how to improve the situation (or solve the problem).
9) If the model does not satisfactorily reproduce the observed problem(s), then the person must go back to the step in which the model was made and revise the model as needed. The remaining steps in the process then must be repeated using the new model. Eventually, the problem solver will find an acceptable solution to the initial problem and the process ends.

From this listing, one may observe that a model is programmed in step 6 with the aid of a flowchart of the logic in the model. While sometimes eliminated as unnecessary, a flowchart is often valuable for constructing a correct computer program of a programmer's logic. The basics of flowcharting are presented in the next section.

1-4 FLOWCHARTING

One of the most important steps in solving any problem by computer is to insure that the set of instructions given to the computer does, in fact, represent the complete desired set of instructions and the correct order for those instructions. If the set of instructions given to the computer is erroneous in any way, then the results returned by the computer will also be erroneous. Sometimes a program will be written to solve one problem and, because of a mistake in the logic of a programmer, will actually solve a different problem. One way to try to insure that the logic is correct is to carefully diagram the sequence of instructions being given to the computer. Such a diagram is called a flowchart.

A flowchart conveys a representation of all major instructions needed to solve a problem. Of equal importance, the flowchart also specifies the correct order in which the instructions are to be carried out. Another advantage of flowcharting is the use of the visual picture that is formed. Often the flowchart can be used to convince oneself or others of the validity of the solution procedure, or algorithm, used.

The construction of a flowchart could be accomplished by simply connecting (with a solid line) short phrases indicating the desired steps in a user's algorithm for solving a problem. For example, if a user wished to use Fortran to put two values into computer memory, add them, and display the summation, one possible simplified flowchart would be:

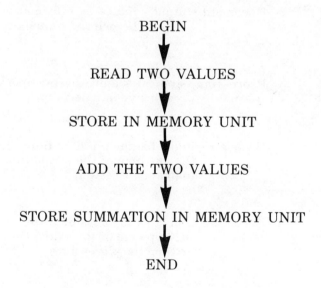

BEGIN

READ TWO VALUES

STORE IN MEMORY UNIT

ADD THE TWO VALUES

STORE SUMMATION IN MEMORY UNIT

END

Many other flowcharts could be constructed for this same general algorithm described above. As a means of standardizing the process of flowchart construction, certain graphical symbols are suggested by the American National Standards Institute (ANSI). A listing of the commonly used symbols and the meaning

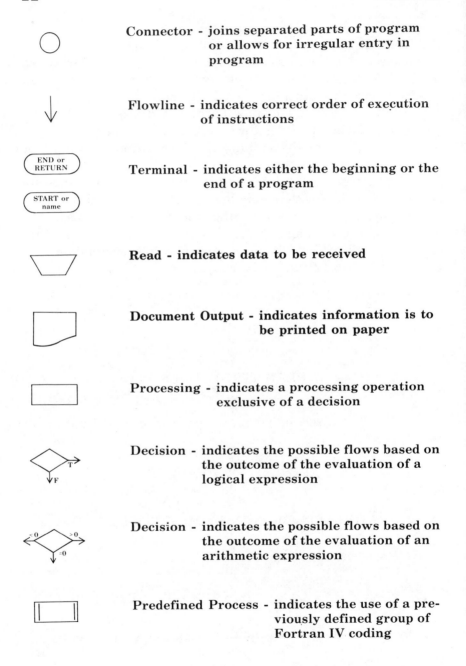

Connector - joins separated parts of program
or allows for irregular entry in
program

Flowline - indicates correct order of execution
of instructions

Terminal - indicates either the beginning or the
end of a program

Read - indicates data to be received

**Document Output - indicates information is to
be printed on paper**

**Processing - indicates a processing operation
exclusive of a decision**

Decision - indicates the possible flows based on
the outcome of the evaluation of a
logical expression

Decision - indicates the possible flows based on
the outcome of the evaluation of an
arithmetic expression

Predefined Process - indicates the use of a previously defined group of
Fortran IV coding

Figure 1-6.
Selected Flowchart Symbols of
American National Standards Institute

of each is given in Fig. 1-6. The above example could have the following flowchart formulation if ANSI flowchart symbols are used:

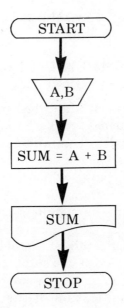

One difference between the two flowcharts is that, by using the ANSI flowchart symbols, a user does not have to incorporate instructions for assigning values to memory. A, B, and SUM are all Fortran labels (since this flowchart is for a Fortran program) that identify certain storage registers in the computer memory; therefore, values associated with these variables are stored in the memory unit — automatically upon initial use of the labels "A", "B", and "SUM".

A user obviously could forego the extra effort expended in preparing a flowchart for the simple set of instructions in the above example. The indicated flow of operations is straightforward, and the flowchart may indeed be considered unnecessary. Thus, flowcharting may seem to be relatively useless and unrewarding to a beginning student in programming. However, most algorithms used in science and engineering involve many complex sets of instructions with decisions, looping, and use of predefined procedures, to name a few. Application of flowcharting techniques in the novice stage of programming will prove rewarding when complex

problems are encountered later and will always help to organize
one's thoughts for program construction. A number of examples of
flowcharts appear in this text. A good reference on flowcharting is
contained in Chap. 7 of *Engineering Fundamentals and Problem
Solving* by Eide, *et al.* (McGraw-Hill Book Co., New York, 1979).

1-5 METHODS OF COMMUNICATING
WITH THE PROCESSOR

The communications system established to this point in Chap. 1
has covered two subsystems:
  (1) The compiler system communicating problem solving
      instructions to the basic machine (via the processor), and
  (2) The user communicating which problem he or she wants
      solved (via flowcharting).
Two additional links in the complete communication system
remain:
  (1) The user's communication of a problem to be solved to the
      processor by means of a computer program (this book
      describes Fortran IV computer programming), and
  (2) Processor communication of the output results of the
      machine performance of instructions and any calculations
      (via output display to the user).
The first of the additional links actually involves programming
and input operations, whereas the second link primarily involves
output operations. Both input and output operations must be
precisely specified by programmed user instructions, just as any
arithmetic or logic operation is specified. Input and output can be
performed through any of a number of devices. As a standard, most
computer facilities provide punched card input and printed paper
output. These means of communication with the computer are often
accompanied by unnecessary time delays and cumbersome
accumulations of punched cards and printed paper. Time-sharing
(sometimes referred to as interactive programming) is one alternative. Paper can still accumulate, and some "hard copies" of final
output are often desirable, but the biggest advantage of its use is
the time savings realized by the programmer.
    In time-sharing, an electric typewriter terminal — perhaps
located at a point distant from the computer itself for easy user
access — allows a user to communicate with the machine. Because

of the high speed of most modern computers, many users may use terminals in rapid sequence, thus "time-share" the computer from different points. The speed of communication often gives the user the illusion of being the only user of the computer.

The use of a computer in a time-sharing mode is similar to punched card entry use of the computer. The programming requirements in Fortran IV are identical except for input/output designations. Special routings (usually not the reader/printer routings as utilized in punched card/printed paper input/output) are made for use of the terminal or auxiliary memory devices on input or output. Data may be entered via the terminal keyboard or from stored material on magnetic tape or other storage devices. Special commands must be used to communicate with the machine itself. These, of course, will vary according to the exact type of machine utilized.

Time-sharing is indeed a more efficient method of communicating with the computer. For financial reasons, some computer users can only afford to operate on a time-sharing basis, and the terminal may be the only form of communication with a computer. In the academic environment, however, time-sharing is usually an alternate method of computer communication and may be most efficiently utilized by students who are working on long, involved problems. Debugging and program modification are more easily accomplished in this way.

The description of the use of terminals in a time-sharing mode on computers is beyond the scope of this text. For an explanation of the use of Fortran in time-sharing, personnel in one's own computer center should be consulted for obtaining literature.

2

Basic Concepts and Features of Fortran

Before learning how to write a Fortran program, one must understand several important concepts. Inasmuch as the authors have attempted to present Fortran in a simple and concise form, the reader is strongly advised to read and study these concepts carefully to avoid missing something that will be important later on.

2-1 TWO KINDS OF NUMBERS

In Fortran programming, it is necessary to distinguish between two kinds of numbers — *integer* (sometimes called "fixed point") *numbers* and *real* (sometimes called "floating point") *numbers*.

"Integers" are whole numbers. They may be either positive, negative, or zero. They must not have a decimal. Examples of integers are

22   -63   0   9   4388   -4388

"Reals" are numbers that have a fractional part (although the fractional part for a particular real number may be zero). They may be either positive, negative, or zero. They must have a decimal. Examples of reals are

22.   -63.0   0.0 4.2×10^8 0.0004   -37652.9

(Commas are not used to separate thousands in Fortran.) The number 4.2×10^8 can be written in Fortran as 4.2E+08.

As a general rule, arithmetic computations in Fortran should be done using real numbers — particularly in engineering applications. With some exceptions, the use of integer numbers in Fortran should be limited to DO parameters (Chap. 6), subscripts (for subscripted variables) (Chap. 6), and computations where items are only counted.

17

An integer number may be transformed into a real number by placing a decimal at its end. When a real number is transformed into an integer number, both the decimal and the fractional part are discarded. Thus 3.98 becomes 3 when transformed.

2-2   CONSTANTS AND VARIABLES

A *constant* is any number that appears in a statement in explicit form. A *variable* is a quantity that is given a name and often allowed to vary in a program. Thus in the statement

JJ = **KK** + **5**

JJ and KK are variables, and 5 is a constant.

There are several rules that must be followed in selecting names for variables. Each variable name must have from one to six alphanumeric characters (i.e., letters and/or digits). The first character must be a letter. No symbols may be used within a variable name. Following these rules, a very large number of acceptable variable names are possible. Examples are

K	JK92	X	RRR444	SEVEN
SUSAN	SCØTT	JØY	JACK	AZ3C
ARK	UNCC	TØMMY	SARAH	SALLIE

(Only upper case letters are used.) The following are unacceptable variable names because of the reasons given:

MATTHEW	**(more than six characters)**
ABC*	**(no symbols allowed)**
7CATS	**(first character must be a letter)**
A+2	**(no symbols allowed)**

Naturally, different variable names must be assigned within a program in order to keep the data separate.

(It will be noted that the letter O (oh) in the variables listed above was shown with a slash mark through it. This is to differentiate it from the number zero. It is also helpful to differentiate between a letter Z (zee) and the number two by forming the letter with a bar through it (Z) and to differentiate between a letter I and the number one by forming the letter with upper and lower bars (I).)

It is necessary to distinguish between variable names that represent an integer number and those that represent a real number. Integer variable names must have as the first character either an I, J, K, L, M, or N. (These may be remembered as the six letters I through N, noting that the letters I and N are the first two letters of the word "integer.") Real variable names must have as the first character any other letter of the alphabet. Only the first character of a variable name has any significance in designating an integer variable or a real variable. Thus in the above list of fifteen acceptable variable names, K, JK92, JØY, and JACK are integer variable names; the remainder are real variable names.

2-3 FORTRAN OPERATIONS

Five basic arithmetic operations are provided in Fortran. Each operation is represented by a symbol. These operations and symbols are as follows:

addition	+
subtraction	-
multiplication	*
division	/
exponentiation	**

No two symbols may appear side by side in a Fortran statement.

2-4 FORTRAN EXPRESSIONS

A Fortran expression consists of one or more constants and/or variables used to compute a numerical value. For example, the expression KK means the value of the integer variable KK; the expression 126.8 means the value of the real constant 126.8; the expression PAL-HAL means the value of the difference between the values of the variables PAL and HAL; and the expression (R-U)/(A+5.0) means the value of the difference between the values of the variables R and U divided by the sum of the variable A and the constant 5.0.

In formulating expressions, parentheses must be used to indicate groupings, as in common mathematical notation. Thus the algebraic expression $c+d^3$ would be written in Fortran notation as C+D**3; whereas the algebraic expression $(c+d)^3$ would be written as (C+D)**3.

If the order of operation is not otherwise defined by parentheses, the hierarchy of operation (sequence in which operations is performed) is as follows: exponentiations are performed first; then multiplications and divisions; and then additions and subtractions.

Thus in the Fortran expression E+F/G-H**5.1, the first operation would be to raise H to the 5.1 power; the second operation would be to divide F by G; and the final operation would be to add (algebraically) the three terms. Whenever parentheses are encountered, the computation within the parentheses is done prior to other computation to reduce the value within to a single number. For example, in the expression (R+S)**3, although exponentiation is normally done first, in this case because of the parentheses, the addition is done first — i.e., R and S are added and then the sum is raised to the power 3. If several terms appear on the same level within an expression, then computation proceeds from left to right (except for exponentiation). Thus in the expression T/U*V, since multiplication and division are on the same level, computation proceeds from left to right and T would be divided by U and the resulting quotient multiplied by V. In the case of exponentiation, however, computation proceeds from right to left in an expression. Thus in the expression F**G**H, the first step would be to raise G to the power H and then F would be raised to that (i.e., G^H) power.

The sequence of operations can, of course, be modified by the use of parentheses, as illustrated by the following:

FORTRAN EXPRESSION	MEANING
E+F/G-H**5.1	$e + \dfrac{f}{g} - h^{5.1}$
(E+F)/G-H**5.1	$\dfrac{e+f}{g} - h^{5.1}$
E+F/(G-II)**5.1	$e + \dfrac{f}{(g-h)^{5.1}}$
E+F/(G-H**5.1)	$e + \dfrac{f}{g-h^{5.1}}$
(E+F)/(G-H)**5.1	$\dfrac{e+f}{(g-h)^{5.1}}$
((E+F)/(G-H))**5.1	$\left[\dfrac{e+f}{g-h}\right]^{5.1}$

Note in the last example that two parentheses are placed side by side. Parentheses are the only means of grouping in Fortran. (There are no brackets or braces.) Therefore, it is often necessary to place two or more pairs of parentheses within an expression in order to clarify the meaning of the expression. Many programming mistakes result from misuse (or lack of use) of parentheses in Fortran expressions. It is generally not harmful to use more parentheses than are necessary, and programmers — particularly inexperienced ones — are encouraged to use parentheses as necessary to eliminate uncertainties. For example, the expression $c/d^{1.7}$ can correctly be written in Fortran as C/D**1.7. The programmer may feel a little more confident, however, in writing C/(D**1.7). It should be emphasized at this point that parentheses must always occur in pairs. When several sets are used in one expression it is wise for **beginners to insure that the number of opening parentheses equals** the number of closing parentheses.

In general, a Fortran expression should not contain both integer numbers and real numbers. This is referred to as "mixed mode." For example, B+2 and AB+K are mixed mode Fortran expressions, since the first term of each is real and the second, integer. The mixed mode can be avoided by making both terms real (B+2.0 and AB+AK) or by making both terms integer (KB+2 and KAB+K). One exception to this rule is that a real value may be raised to an integer power. Thus (A+B+4.2)**5 and (15.5/R)**(J+2) are valid expressions.

As stated above, mixed mode should generally be avoided. However, in some instances mixed mode may be used to advantage by experienced programmers. Results of mixed mode arithmetic are, however, sometimes unexpected, and the novice programmer is strongly urged to avoid it. For example, if A=100.0, the statement, Y=A*(2/3), would give Y a value of zero. (This is true because the 2 and the 3 within the parentheses are both integers; and when the 2 is divided by the 3, the division is done in "integer arithmetic," meaning that fractional parts are always discarded. Thus 2 divided by 3 is, in this instance, zero, giving Y a value of zero.) To avoid this mixed mode, the statement may be written as Y=A*(2./3.). Mixed mode expressions also take longer to evaluate than expressions written properly. Thus the statement, X=2*A/3, takes almost twice as many operations as the statement, X=2.0*A/3.0. Most new programmers are not used to placing decimals after whole numbers, but they should get into the habit of doing so when writing real numbers in Fortran programs. Many problems beginners have with Fortran result from failure to distinguish properly between integer and real numbers and variables.

2-5 ARITHMETIC ASSIGNMENT STATEMENTS

The first of several "Fortran statements" will be introduced in this chapter. Additional Fortran statements will be introduced as needed in subsequent chapters. The statement to be introduced here is called the *arithmetic assignment statement*, and it is useful in computing a new value of a variable. It takes the general form a=b, where "a" is a variable name (and nothing else) and "b" is any Fortran expression. When an arithmetic assignment statement is the numerical value of the expression on the right is computed, and this value is assigned to the variable on the left.

As an example of an arithmetic assignment statement, consider

   Y = A+4.2

If this statement is executed in a Fortran program, the numerical value of the expression on the right (A+4.2) will be computed, and this value will be assigned to the variable on the left. At execution time, it is necessary that A has previously been given some value. Suppose the value of A has previously been determined as 10.0. Upon execution of the Fortran statement above, the value of the expression on the right would be computed to be 14.2. This value of 14.2 would then be assigned to the variable on the left (Y) and would wipe out the previous value of Y (if one existed). After execution of this statement, the value of A (and any other variables on the right side of the equal sign) remains unchanged. Y would continue to have the value of 14.2 unless it is replaced by another numerical value. The reader should keep in mind that in a Fortran program a variable can have only one numerical value at any one time.

It is possible (and frequently occurs) that the variable name on the left may appear in the expression on the right. If this occurs, the *last assigned value* of that variable is used to compute the value of the expression on the right, and this computed value of the expression is assigned to the variable on the left (thereby wiping out the previously assigned value). For example, suppose the variable JKL has been assigned the value of 8, and the statement JKL = JKL+2 is to be executed. The last assigned value of JKL is 8, and this will be added to the constant 2, giving the value of the expression on the right as 10. The new value of 10 is now assigned to the variable JKL. If this statement is executed again, the last assigned value of JKL, which is now 10, will be added to the constant 2, giving the value of the expression on the right as 12. The new value of 12 is now assigned to the variable JKL.

It should be emphasized that the statement JKL = JKL+2 is not an "equation" in the normal, mathematical sense of the word, although it does contain an equal sign. (If it were, JKL could be subtracted from both sides, leaving 0 = 2, which is an interesting non-fact.) It is an arithmetic assignment statement, where "assignment" means "value is stored at that address." Thus a Fortran equal sign (=) means "replaced by." This distinction is a very important one in Fortran.

It has been stated (Sec. 2-4) that it is not advisable to mix real numbers and integer numbers in an expression. It is possible, however, to have an expression of one mode on the right side of an arithmetic assignment statement and a variable of the other mode on the left. If this occurs, the arithmetic in computing the value of the expression on the right will be done in the mode used in the expression. The computed value of the expression will be converted to the other mode before it is assigned to the variable on the left. For example, suppose A has the value 3.8 and the following statement is executed.

MM = 2. * A

Clearly the variable on the left is integer, while the expression on the right is real. In execution, real arithmetic on the right would yield the value of the expression as 7.6. This real value would be converted to an integer value, and the integer value would be assigned to the variable on the left. Thus, in this example, MM would take the value 7. Note that the value 7.6 is not rounded up. As related in Sec. 2-1, when a real number is transformed into an integer number, both the decimal point and the fractional part are discarded. This is called truncation.

2-6 BUILT-IN FUNCTIONS

"Functions," as used in Fortran, will be covered in detail in Chap. 7. There are, however, built-in functions in Fortran that can be quite useful in routine programming — particularly in engineering applications. Some of the most frequently used ones are presented in this section.

One type of function that is frequently used in engineering applications is the various trigonometric functions. Sine, cosine, and tangent functions are available in Fortran. The names of these functions are SIN, CØS, and TAN respectively. To use these functions, one must write down the name of the function followed by an expression in parentheses, where the expression when evaluated gives the angle whose sine or cosine is required. When using these trigonometric functions, the angles must be expressed in radians.

As an example, assume it is desired to compute the cosine of 39°52'. This could be done in Fortran using the following arithmetic assignment statement:

C=CØS((39.+52./60.)*3.14159265/180.)

Note that the angle is first converted from units of degrees and minutes to units of degrees (with fractional parts) only and is then converted to radians. All of this is done within the parentheses immediately following the function name CØS; hence, the cosine of the angle expressed in radians will be determined and assigned to the variable C.

Only the sine, cosine, and tangent trigonometric functions are available in Fortran, but other trigonometric functions can be evaluated in terms of these two. For example, suppose an angle identified in a program as BETA has been evaluated in radians, and it is desired to determine the sum of the cotangent of this angle and the secant of this angle. This could be done in Fortran using appropriate trigonometric identities as shown in the following arithmetic assignment statement:

S=1./TAN(BETA)+1./CØS(BETA)

Table 2-1 gives a list of some of the most often used built-in functions available in Fortran.

Function Name	Meaning
SQRT	square root
ABS	absolute value
EXP	exponential
ALØG	natural logarithm
ALØG10	base 10 logarithm
SIN	sine
CØS	cosine
TAN	tangent
ASIN	arcsine
ACØS	arccosine
ATAN	arctangent
SINH	hyperbolic sine
CØSH	hyperbolic cosine
TANH	hyperbolic tangent

Note: In the last nine functions involving angles, the angle is expressed in radians.

Table 2 - 1

It should be emphasized that Table 2 - 1 gives only a partial listing of available functions. A more complete list is given in Appendix A. It should also be emphasized that, because of some variation in Fortran compilers, some of the functions listed in Table 2 - 1 and Appendix A may not be available in some Fortran compilers. To use any of these functions, one must write down the name of the function followed by an expression in parentheses. This expression when evaluated must give the value, the function of which is desired.

2-7 PROBLEMS

2-1 Which of the following are real numbers and which are integer numbers?

−29	18.5	2×10^7	2×10^{-7}	5.0
−1.1	−1	0	16	−16
−0.7	$.28 \times 10^{-4}$	100.	10000	80.0

2-2 Transform the following integer numbers into real numbers.

26	50	0	−500	88

2-3 Transform the following real numbers into integer numbers (as the computer would).

42.	89.0	−32.2	−298.7	0.99999

2-4   Which of the following are valid variable names?

A	AA7	7AA	BØØK	BOOK
IBARGAIN	B*A	M9M	Z2	ØO
IJKLMN	101	Ø42	JBUGJJ	OØ

2-5   Which of the variables listed above (Problem 2-4) are valid integer variables?

In each of Problems 2-6 through 2-9, write a Fortran statement for the equation given using all *real* variables.

2-6
$$x = ai + \frac{bk}{m} - \frac{(a+b)^{n+1}}{a+b^{n+1}}$$

2-7
$$r = \left[\frac{a}{(t+u)^n - w}\right]^{b+5} - b/cd$$

2-8 $j = kar^{n+1} - u + w^2 - 1/(a+b)$

2-9
$$m = \left[\frac{a+b+i}{j-(k-20)^t}\right]^{0.66} \div (r+t)^{5.5}$$

In each of the Problems 2-10 through 2-14 tell what, if anything, is wrong (illegal) with the arithmetic assignment statement given.

2-10   K = A*B*C ** D/20.2 + CØS (A - B)

2-11   AL = 0.5 * (A - B) ** - 3

2-12   R = A/B * C - 10.2/(D/E) ** 2F

2-13   B + 2 = 4. * AC ** A * C/GGG ** 5.1

2-14   N = A - B - 77.7 ** A/2.0

In each of the Problems 2-15 through 2-20 evaluate (using a calculator) the expression given if A = 5.5, B = 6.9, C = 0.42, and D = -0.0333.

2-15   A/B - C ** D

2-16   (C - D)/A + B

2-17   B * C/D * A

2-18   (B-C-A) ** C/2.0

2-19   3.3 * D/(5.1 + C) * A

2-20   A ** 5.9 ** C

2-21   A farmer owns a piece of property that is triangular in shape. She measured the lengths of the sides of the property and recorded the following results: 817 ft, 996 ft, and 777 ft. Write an arithmetic assignment statement that will compute the area (in acres) of this piece of property. (There are 43,560 ft^2 in one acre.)

2-22 Professor I.M. Happy has a class of five students. She gave a quiz to these students and wants to find the average of the five quiz grades. Write an arithmetic assignment statement that will compute the average of five quiz grades.

3
Input/Output

As stated in Chap. 1, a major part of the process of utilizing the capabilities of a computer is the ability to transfer information to the computer and to receive some feedback of the results of using that information in some way. For example, if it is desired to find the average value for five readings from a controlled experiment, one would have to develop a Fortran program to somehow receive the five readings, average them, and then display the average value. In this chapter the various methods by which a program can receive and display information will be examined. The reader should realize that data may be communicated not only to display units but also to storage units. This chapter is primarily devoted to output of data by display units and typical input of data by the user.

3-1 OUTPUT STATEMENTS

The arithmetic assignment statement (Sec. 2-5) can be used to compute results needed by the programmer, but some method must be available to pass these results from the computer back to the programmer. Thus this section will examine the "computer-to-programmer" communications necessary to display results — that is, the *Fortran output statement*. Output may be requested at any point in a program through the use of an output statement. An output statement may be of the following form:

WRITE(m,n)list

The word WRITE indicates that the results of the execution of part of a program are to be made available for use elsewhere. Again, concern here will be with the display of the results for user inspection. The output will be transferred usually either to paper at a printer or to the screen of a cathode-ray tube (CRT). The exact destination of output is controlled by the user for his or her convenience. Output material commonly is transferred to paper so that it may be used by others or examined at later dates.

The letters "m" and "n" in the generalized output statement above represent integer numbers, which must be supplied by the programmer. The "m" integer is chosen to indicate the programmer's computer center code for the device that is to receive the transferred material. For illustration purposes, the integer 6 will be used in this book for "m" for all WRITE statements. This number often is used to identify the high-speed line printer or CRT terminal as the device to receive (and display) output. The "n" integer is the label for the Fortran statement that indicates how the information is to appear on output. This statement is called a FØRMAT statement, and it will be described in detail in the next section of this chapter. Briefly, as the word indicates, the FØRMAT statement contains the programmer's specific directions for the layout of output when referenced by a WRITE statement.

The list that is found in a WRITE statement is a collection of all of the variable names whose values have been defined in a program and are to be transferred as output from the program. The list may include any previously defined variable names in any order desired.

As an illustration of a complete WRITE statement, consider:

WRITE(6,20)ANS,NUM,XYƵ,I38,B,DØG

Note that the first number in parentheses is a 6 — indicating (it will be assumed) that output is to be printed by the high-speed line printer. The second number indicates that FØRMAT statement number 20 provides the directions for display of output by the printer. The list in this example contains six variable names. These names are separated by commas, with no comma before or after the list. The value stored in the memory location corresponding to each variable name in the list is to be printed according to the dictates of FØRMAT statement 20. Note that the list in the example contains real variables ANS,XYZ,B, and DØG, as well as integer variables NUM and I38. The list may contain any type of Fortran variable as long as the referenced FØRMAT statement is in agreement with the individual elements in the list.

In the general WRITE statement, the only optional element is the list. Sometimes a programmer wishes to print only messages or headings on an output sheet. In these instances, a WRITE statement may be used without a list of variable names. The only material to be printed as output would appear in the referenced FØRMAT statement.

3-2 FØRMAT STATEMENTS

Maintaining the agreement that must exist between the list of a WRITE statement and a FØRMAT statement is an important responsibility of the programmer. Every FØRMAT statement is composed of FØRMAT entry designations, which are used to insure the exact desired presentation of the output. The general form of a FØRMAT statement is:

n FØRMAT(e1, e2, e3,...)

In this form, "n" represents the statement number of the FØRMAT statement. For this statement to be utilized on output, the number "n" must be the second integer in the parentheses of some WRITE statement. Every FØRMAT statement within a given program must have a unique statement number. Each variable in the list of a WRITE statement is associated with one of the entries (e1, e2, e3,...) in the parentheses following the word FØRMAT.

If a variable referred to in the WRITE list is integer, the associated entry in the FØRMAT statement takes the form "Iw". The "I" designates the entry as an integer FØRMAT designation. The "w" is an integer used here to indicate the number of spaces or positions in which the value of the integer variable is to be placed. One space should be allowed for the sign of the number to be displayed. For example, in the previous WRITE statement, assume the variable named NUM has a value of 245 at the time the WRITE statement is executed. An acceptable FØRMAT designation to be associated with the variable NUM would be "I4". The "I" designates an integer variable; the "4" indicates that four spaces will be set aside in which to print the value 245. Note that one extra space has been provided for the sign of the value of NUM. (If the sign of the value to be printed is positive, a plus sign will not be printed.) Frequently, the exact sign or size of the value being printed will not be known by the programmer when the FØRMAT statements are constructed. In such cases it is wise to use a FØRMAT entry designation that is somewhat larger than the estimated largest value of the variable. In any case, the value to be printed will appear in the right-most portion of the space provided (i.e., will be right-justified in the total number of spaces provided for its printing). Any blank spaces will appear in the left portion of the total "w" spaces provided. Thus, in the previous example, if the value of NUM was unknown, a format entry designation of I8 could be specified. In this case the value 245 would be printed preceded by five blank spaces.

If the variable referred to in the WRITE list is real, the associated entry in the FØRMAT statement may take the form "Fw.d". The "F" designates the entry as a real FØRMAT designation. The "w" is a number that indicates how many spaces are to be allowed within which the value is to be printed. One space should be allowed for the sign of the printed number, and one space has to be allowed for the decimal that is printed. The "d" indicates how many digits to the right of the decimal are to be printed. (Note that w should exceed d by 2 or more.) Thus the programmer can control the number of decimal places of a variable's value that will be printed. For example, suppose the variable ANS with a value of -17.28 is to be printed. An acceptable FØRMAT entry designation would be F6.2. The "F" is appropriate because ANS is a real variable. The "6" indicates that six spaces will be required to print the value -17.28. The "2" indicates that the first two digits of the decimal fraction of the value of ANS will be printed.

Consider again the WRITE statement used in Sec. 3-1 and an appropriate FØRMAT statement:

WRITE(6,20)ANS,NUM,XYƵ,I38,B,DØG
20 FØRMAT(F10.2,I4,F8.0,I6,F6.3,F6.3)

Note that 20 in the WRITE statement corresponds to the statement number 20 of the FØRMAT statement. In this example, also note that there is one entry in the FØRMAT statement for each variable in the WRITE statement list. The F10.2 designation is associated with the variable ANS. Thus the value of variable ANS is intended to be printed in the first ten spaces on the print line, and there are to be two digits to the right of the decimal. The decimal itself will occupy one of the ten spaces. The I4 in the FØRMAT statement is associated with the variable NUM. The value stored in the variable location named NUM will be printed in the next four spaces on the print line. The rest of the variables in the WRITE statement will, of course, be associated with the remaining FØRMAT entry designations in the FØRMAT statement.

When two or more consecutive identical entries appear in a FØRMAT statement, the following shortcut may be employed:

20 FØRMAT(F10.2,I4,F8.0,I6,2F6.3)

Thus the entries associated with the variables B and DØG in the previous example are represented by 2F6.3 — the "2" indicating two identical entries of F6.3. This FØRMAT statement is equivalent to the previous one.

The actual location of a FØRMAT statement may be at any point in a program listing prior to the END statement (the END statement is explained in Chap. 4). Since the FØRMAT is not an executable Fortran statement, its placement is not important as is the placement of executable statements. Some programmers place FØRMAT statements in groups either at the beginning of the Fortran program or at the end. Another factor to consider in the use of FØRMAT statements is that more than one output (and/or input) statement may refer to the same FØRMAT statement. Thus every WRITE statement need not refer to a separate FØRMAT statement. Of course, there still must be agreement between variables in the WRITE (and/or READ) list and entries in the FØRMAT statement for all WRITE (and/or READ) statements that reference a particular FØRMAT statement.

Real variables in a WRITE list may also be associated with FØRMAT entries of the form "Ew.d", where "E" refers to the fact that the value of the real variable is to be printed in a form similar to scientific notation. As indicated previously, the "w" refers to the number of print positions that will be required for the total display of a value. This includes one space for the sign of the value, one space for the letter E, two for the characteristic (exponent from the scientific notation form of the value), one space for the sign of the characteristic, "d" spaces for the mantissa of the value, one space for the decimal point in the mantissa, and one space for a zero in the digit's position. (Note that w should exceed d by 7 or more.)

To illustrate, suppose the value of the real variable XYƵ was to be printed. If XYƵ had a value of -23,346,000,000., one could request that this value be printed using the E FØRMAT. An acceptable FØRMAT entry designation that could be associated with variable XYƵ is E12.5. The output from the computer would look something like this:

-0.23346E+11

Note that the output uses a total of 12 spaces and that there are five digits to the right of the decimal in the mantissa (.23346). Since the value given for XYƵ here is equivalent to 0.23346×10^{11}, the exponent "11" is shown to the right of "E" on output. Thus the above output is in agreement with the FØRMAT entry designation E12.5.

A fourth type of FØRMAT entry designation is the "A" designation. This can be used to print letters, symbols, and/or numbers as characters. The FØRMAT designation must be of the general form "Aw", where "w" is an integer number that indicates the number of spaces in which the value of the variable is to be written out. The "w" in this case may take on only a limited number of values. Most Fortran compilers will accept a maximum width of four (w=4); some will accept as many as six (w=6). With some compilers, variables can be assigned letters, symbols, and/or numbers as values through the use of arithmetic assignment statements. Single quote marks must be used as follows:

   Y='WØRD'

Note that the single quotes are used here to enclose the characters WØRD. Such characters can also be assigned to variables by using the DATA statement or the READ statement and associated FØRMAT statement (see Sec. 3-3).

If the value of Y appeared in a WRITE list after the above statement, a FØRMAT entry designation of A4 would be required to be associated with the variable Y. An acceptable WRITE/FØRMAT combination would appear as:

   WRITE(6,100)Y
   100 FØRMAT(1X,A4)

(In this example, 1X is another FØRMAT entry designation that will be described next.)

Two additional FØRMAT designations, which are useful in spacing output, are "X" and "T". Their general forms are "nX" and "Tn" respectively, where "n" is an unsigned integer constant. The "n" used with an "X" designation means to skip positions or spaces. In the last example, FØRMAT statement 100 included a 1X designation. This was used to indicate that the first print position would be skipped — thus it would contain a blank. The "T" FØRMAT designation is used like a "tab" key on a typewriter. The integer following "T" indicates the print position to skip to prior to printing any succeeding data. Note the difference between "X" and "T". "X" skips a certain number of spaces; whereas "T" skips to a particular space. As an example, consider the following:

   WRITE(6,95)A,B,C,J
   95 FØRMAT(T3,F5.2,5X,F6.3,T32,F10.2,5X,I6)

In this example, the value of A is intended to appear in columns 3 through 7; B, in columns 13 through 18; C, in columns 32 through 41; and J, in columns 47 through 52.

At this point the computer's process of readying data to be printed should be examined briefly. Output is prepared in conjunction with user instructions (using the WRITE and FØRMAT statements in Fortran). Each line is stored until such time as the computer operations dictate specific output is to be printed — sometimes immediately; sometimes much later. The WRITE/FØRMAT combinations are user instructions for the composition of lines of characters for output. Each line that is composed by WRITE/FØRMAT combinations is called an output *record*. Additionally, the Fortran compiler associates the character in the first position of each record as a carriage control command. This command can be generally one of four:

Character	Vertical Spacing on Printer
blank	advance to next line
0	skip one line
1	skip to top of new page
+	do not advance

Thus in the last WRITE/FØRMAT example, FØRMAT statement 95 actually provided a blank as the carriage control command, since nothing was indicated to appear in column 1 of the output record. The values of A, B, C, and J would appear on the next line of output for the program in which these values appeared. The carriage control command is not printed as output; thus the actual location of the values of A, B, C, and J would appear in the *printed* positions 2 through 51 (as opposed to *record* positions 3 through 52). Also, in the next to last WRITE/FØRMAT example, the 1X of FØRMAT statement 100 was included to provide a blank as the carriage control command.

The programmer must insure that the intended carriage control command is relayed to the computer via the first character of every output record. To illustrate this concept, consider the following:

```
      A=1.42
      WRITE(6,145)A
  145 FØRMAT(1X,F6.2)
      WRITE(6,146)A
  146 FØRMAT(F6.2)
      WRITE(6,147)A
  147 FØRMAT(F4.2)
```

If this group of statements was executed at the beginning of a Fortran program, the following output would result:

Printed Position	1	2	3	4	5	6	7	8	9
Print Line #1			1	.	4	2			
Print Line #2		1	.	4	2				
Print Line #1 (on next page)	.	4	2						

FØRMAT statement 145 had a blank carriage control character; thus the output generated by the first WRITE statement began on the next line with two blanks preceding 1.42 in the printed positions. The 1X format entry was used specifically to transmit the blank carriage control command. When the second WRITE statement was executed, the carriage control command was actually included as part of the FØRMAT entry designation associated with the variable A. Since the value of A (1.42) only required 4 of the 6 spaces indicated by F6.2, two blanks precede 1.42 in the output record position. In this case, the first blank is the carriage control command, and thus the second set of output appears on the next print line with only one blank preceding 1.42 in the printed positions. When the third WRITE statement was executed, the carriage control command was again included as part of the FØRMAT entry designation associated with the variable A. Since the value of A (1.42) requires 4 spaces and the FØRMAT entry F4.2 allows for only 4 total spaces, the digit 1 in the number 1.42 becomes the carriage control; hence, the third set of output appears on the first line of the next page. Additionally, the digit 1 in the number 1.42 does not get printed. In all likelihood, this (third) example of WRITE/FØRMAT and associated output would be very undesirable in a program. This latter example underscores the necessity that whenever an output record is being formulated by a programmer, he or she should be aware that whatever character appears in the first position for each FØRMAT statement will be considered the carriage control command. This character will not be printed.

Examples of FØRMAT statements heretofore have involved an exact correspondence between the number of variables in a WRITE list and the number of variable FØRMAT entry designations. This situation is generally the best method for output, but variations may exist, which provide some degree of flexibility in the composition of WRITE/FØRMAT statements. For example, consider this:

WRITE(6,45)A,B,C
45 FØRMAT(1X,F2.0,F6.3,F4.1,I6,F4.1)

FØRMAT statement 45 contains five FØRMAT designations for variables — yet the WRITE list contains only three variables. In this case, variable A is associated with F2.0; variable B, with F6.3; and variable C, with the first F4.1. The last two FØRMAT designations (I6 and the second F4.1) will not be used by the WRITE statement given.

Suppose that the WRITE statement list had contained more elements than there were FØRMAT entries in the associated FØRMAT statement. How would this situation be handled? There are many different possibilities that could exist that are correct. One situation might involve the following:

WRITE(6,150)A,B,C,D,E
150 FØRMAT(1X,F6.2)

The variable A will be associated with F6.2 as usual. As the Fortran compiler tries to associate a FØRMAT designation with B, the closing right parenthesis is encountered in the FØRMAT statement. This causes the Fortran compiler to return to the first left parenthesis that is encountered in moving from the closing parenthesis in the FØRMAT statement. Here the only left parenthesis is the opening one. Thus the compiler will "start over" in referencing FØRMAT statement 150. B will be associated with F6.2 also; likewise, C, D, and E will all be associated with F6.2. Not until all elements in the WRITE list have been associated with a FØRMAT entry designation will the execution of a WRITE statement end. In other words, values for all variables in the list in the WRITE statement will be printed (assuming no programming errors exist).

One point to note in the last example is that the closing right parenthesis of the FØRMAT statement also designates the end of the output record. The above WRITE statement thus generated five output records. Each record had the same FØRMAT — 1X and F6.2. Thus the carriage control command for each record was a blank (1X). The values for variables A, B, C, D, and E would appear on a print sheet on five consecutive lines, with a different value on each line. In other words, each time the FØRMAT is "repeated" in this case, a new line of output results. Thus A, B, C, D, and E would be printed as a column.

One other possible variation for the previous example could be:

WRITE(6,155)A,B,C,D,E
155 FØRMAT(1X,2(2X,F6.2,3X,F4.1))   (First)

In this FØRMAT statement, an illustration is given of a repetitive group of FØRMAT designations. The interior set of parentheses bounds a portion of FØRMAT entry designations that are to be repeated — twice in this instance. The above FØRMAT statement 155 could be restated as follows:

155 FØRMAT(1X,2X,F6.2,3X,F4.1,2X,F6.2,3X,F4.1)   (Second)

The FØRMAT statements themselves would be equivalent; however, execution of the above WRITE statement with reference to the first FØRMAT statement would cause the values for A, B, C, D, and E to be printed in a slightly different layout than when the second FØRMAT statement is referenced.

The sequence followed in the execution of the WRITE statement above with the *first* FØRMAT statement 155 is:

1. The first output record has a blank carriage control character ("1X").
2. A is associated with F6.2.
3. B is associated with F4.1.
4. First right parenthesis is encountered; a repeat is made of designations in interior parentheses (to satisfy the group count of 2).
5. C is associated with F6.2.
6. D is associated with F4.1.
7. First right parenthesis is encountered again and group count is satisfied; thus the second right parenthesis is encountered.
8. Since this is the closing right parenthesis for FØRMAT

statement 155, the end of an output record has been reached.

9. The compiler now returns to the first left parenthesis that is encountered. This is the left parenthesis for the repeated group. (The group count of 2 is reused if necessary in satisfying the WRITE list.)

10. The formulation of a new output record is begun at this point and a carriage control is sought for this output record (so that the value of variable E may be printed).

11. The first blank space indicated by the "2X" FØRMAT entry designation is used as the carriage control for the next output record.

12. E is associated with F6.2.

13. The WRITE list is satisfied.

14. Execution of the WRITE statement is completed.

The values of variables A, B, C, and D would be printed on one line. The value of variable E would be printed on the following line.

If the *second* FØRMAT statement 155 was used, the only difference in the output would be that the carriage control character for the second output record would come from the FØRMAT entry designation "1X".

Again, the values for A, B, C, and D would appear on one line, and E's value would appear on the next line. The reader should verify this to assure complete understanding.

Another FØRMAT editing feature is the slash (/). When a slash appears in a FØRMAT statement, it means that a record is to be terminated. To demonstrate, consider the following example:

WRITE(6,999)XY,TV
999 FØRMAT(1X,F7.2/T4,F8.0)

In this example, the value of XY would appear in columns 1 through 7 of the next line of print; the value of TV would appear in columns 3 through 10 on the following line of output.

Up to this point, only the values of variables or blank spaces have been treated as possible printed output. It is usually, however, more desirable to have the output described in some way — with headings, labels, or whatever. In this way anyone — not just the programmer — can identify the output and possibly use it. (Even the programmer can forget the meaning of the output if he or she returns to it later.)

Any desired information — numbers, characters, or words — may be printed by enclosing the information within apostrophes. For example, suppose one wished to print the name Alfred. This could be done as follows:

WRITE(6,345)
345 FØRMAT('   ALFRED')

Note that the WRITE statement contains no list, since no values of variables were desired. Note also that FØRMAT 345 contains only the information desired to be printed inside the apostrophes. Where is the carriage control command? The command is also included inside the apostrophes in the form of the first of the three leading blanks. Thus the word ALFRED would be printed in columns 3 through 8 of the next output line.

Output of the type indicated in the FØRMAT above could also be printed using an "H" FØRMAT entry designation. When "H" appears in a FØRMAT, the (alphanumeric) characters following it will be written on the output, provided an integer number is placed in front of the "H". This integer indicates how many characters following the "H" are to be written. Thus the FØRMAT above could also have been written as

345 FØRMAT(9H   ALFRED)

Descriptive output can also be used in the same WRITE/FØRMAT statements in which the values of variables are being printed. Suppose the sum of several numbers has been computed and assigned to the variable SUM. The value of the variable SUM can be meaningfully printed by the following:

WRITE(6,68)SUM
68 FØRMAT('   THE SUM IS',F10.2)

If the value of the computed sum had been 48216.16, the output would be:

Printed Position

1 2 3 4 5 6 7 8 9 10 11 12 13 14 15 16 17 18 19 20 21 22
T H E   S U M   I S   4 8 2 1 6 . 1 6

The characters inside the apostrophes would be printed as shown. The F10.2 designation is associated with the variable SUM from the WRITE list in the usual manner.

As mentioned previously, headings could be printed in a similar manner. Careful coordination would be required with the succeeding

WRITE/FØRMAT statement to insure proper alignment of data beneath headings. Care must also be exercised to insure that such column headings are printed only *once* at the top of the columns.

Two final considerations are necessary at this point. Obviously, the number of columns available for printing a single line of output is not unlimited. It is the programmer's responsibility to determine the maximum number of positions or columns that a print record may have on a particular system and to insure that all FØRMAT statements are composed accordingly. Many line printers allow for 132 positions per record; however, some allow 85, 120, 144, etc. The following would not produce the desired results because the number of columns required would exceed the print record length:

    WRITE(6,10)A,J,F,W,T
10 FØRMAT(1X,T40,F20.2,10X,I11,3F25.2)

The second final consideration can be demonstrated by the following example:

    H=314.23
    WRITE(6,725)H
725 FØRMAT(' ',F5.2)

In this example, the value of H cannot be expressed with an "F" FØRMAT entry designation in which the number of positions to the right of the decimal is two and the total width is five columns. Including the decimal, the value of H would require seven (including one space for the unprinted sign) total print positions. This condition might be created by a programmer's mistake and would not produce the output desired. Some compilers would generate an error condition; others would simply print five asterisks instead of any numbers. (If the FØRMAT designation F5.2 is changed to F5.1, a value of H of 314.2 would be written out, however.)

3-3 DATA INPUT

The information used in a program may be received in a number of ways. Three of these methods will be examined in detail. These are:

    1. The arithmetic assignment statement
    2. The DATA statement
    3. The READ statement

The arithmetic assignment statement was introduced in Chap. 2. This statement may be used in two ways. A variable may be

assigned a value that is to be maintained for the duration of the
program. This is convenient for certain constants. For example,
consider the following:

   PI=3.14159265

By this statement a value of π to eight decimal places is stored in
the variable location named PI. Probably PI will not be assigned
any other value by the program in which it is to be used. PI's value
could be used many times in the same program without being
changed as shown in the following two statements:

   CIRCUM=2.0*PI*1.5
   AREA=PI*1.5*1.5

These statements compute the circumference and area, respectively, of a circle of radius 1.5 units. PI does not change but behaves
as a true constant.

A second use of the arithmetic assignment statement is to
assign (or to reassign) a value to a variable either by replacement
with another constant (PI=3.14) or as the result of the evaluation of
an arithmetic expression. The value of the variable AREA was
assigned one value through evaluating the arithmetic expression
"PI*1.5*1.5." AREA could be assigned another value as a result of
evaluating "PI*2.0*2.0" at a different location in the program.

Thus the assignment statement can be used to input values for
variables through executable program statements. Each assignment requires a separate statement and the only way to change the
assignment that occurs is to change at least one statement. This
program change may be costly since the entire program would have
to be compiled again every time a change is made.

The *DATA statement* is a convenient method of providing the
initial values of variables. This statement is non-executable and
generally appears at the beginning of the program listing. It takes
the following form:

   DATA name/value/

where "name" is the variable or variables to be initialized and
"value" is the set of constants to be assigned to the set of variables.
Consider this example:

   DATA PI,A,I/3.14159265,2.67,8/

Accordingly, PI is assigned the value 3.14159265; A, the value of
2.67; and I, the value 8. These assignments occur prior to the execu-

tion of any statements in the program. Thus these constitute initial values for variables PI, A, and I.

The following statement would be equivalent to the above example:

DATA PI/3.14159265/,A/2.67/,I/8/

Another equivalent result could be achieved by:

DATA PI/3.14159265/
DATA A/2.67/
DATA I/8/

In Section 3-2, the value WØRD was assigned to the variable Y using an arithmetic assignment statement. Many compilers will not assign letters, numbers, and/or symbols in this manner. A DATA statement may be used as follows:

DATA Y/'WØRD'/

This assignment may also be made using a READ statement and associated "A" FØRMAT.

The arithmetic assignment statement and the DATA statement are useful for a number of situations in which data must be introduced to a program. Often, however, a programmer does not have a predefined initial value for each variable in his or her program. Frequently, programs are designed to utilize various sets of data, which are supplied by the programmer as the program is executed by the computer. Various applications of the same program logic may be applied to the different sets of data without having to reconstruct the program.

The READ statement allows a programmer to have values assigned to variables at the time the READ statement is executed (as opposed to when the program is written). Consider the following illustration:

R=23.4

When included in a Fortran program, this assignment statement indicates that the first value R is assigned in the program would be 23.4. This assignment would always take place for each execution of this statement. A READ statement could allow R to take on values that are supplied upon successive executions of the program. The flexibility gained of course makes the program more widely applicable.

The READ statement is used to introduce data into a program

from sources external to the program. The general form of this input statement is:

READ(m,n)list

In this form, the key word READ must be followed by two numbers in parentheses and a list. The first number ("m") will represent the external source of the data to be transmitted. This number is associated with a specific device that is capable of storing or originating data. Each computer center determines which numbers are associated with the devices. For example, if "m" is 5, then the 5 might signify that the source of data needed to execute the READ statement is the card reader. (This will be assumed for all READ statements in this book.) If so, data on cards should be supplied by the programmer when submitting the program. Other external sources of data include tape devices, disc drums, and interactive terminals. These sources could all be specified by different values for "m" in READ statements. As with the WRITE statement, the second number ("n") is the label of a FØRMAT statement similar to that previously described. The FØRMAT statement in this case describes the size and location of each data element on a unit input record. For input by punched cards, a unit record would be characters on an 80-column card; via a terminal this would be characters from a 72 column line. In either case, each FØRMAT statement refers to the exact appearance of data on one or more input records. The list in the READ statement refers to the variables whose values are to be assigned — just as the WRITE list can refer to variables whose values are to be printed.

Most of what was stated previously with regard to WRITE/FØRMAT statements applies also to READ/FØRMAT statements. For example, if there are more variables in the list to be assigned than there are FØRMAT entry designations, values will be assigned until the rightmost (closing) parenthesis is encountered in the FØRMAT statement. This would signal the end of the input record — an 80-column card here — and the next input record will be sought. The Fortran compiler will, as stated earlier, search for the first left parenthesis that is encountered in a right to left scan of the FØRMAT statement. At this point the assignment continues with the first FØRMAT entry designations following the indicated left parenthesis. Assignments continue until all variables in the READ list have been assigned.

Examine the following:

READ(5,100)I,J,K
100 FØRMAT(I5)

These statements would require the value for I to be taken from the first five columns of the *first* data card; the value for J, from the first five columns of the *second* data card; and the value for K, from the first five columns of the *third* data card. Suppose statement 100 was changed to:

100 FØRMAT(2I5)

The value for I would come from the first five columns of the first data card as before, but the value for J would be taken from columns 6 through 10 of the first data card. Then the value for K would come from the first five columns of the second data card. What execution would occur if statement 100 was changed to:

100 FØRMAT(10I5)

It is, of course, the programmer's responsibility to know how the data will be read and to arrange the data on the cards correctly. Otherwise, data may be assigned incorrectly, and incorrect answers are sure to result.

When reading data using an I FØRMAT, the data must be positioned to the right of the field ("right adjusted" within the columns designated) on the data card. For example, if the number 26 is to be read from a data card using a designation of I4 (indicating card columns 1 through 4), then the number 26 must be placed in columns 3 and 4. If the 26 was placed in columns 2 and 3, then a zero would be assumed in column 4, and the value assigned would be 260.

When a real variable is being assigned a value (using an "F" FØRMAT entry designation), the data do not necessarily have to be positioned according to the entry designation. The number must appear in the data field indicated by the width of the field ("w" from "Fw.d"), but if a decimal is punched on the data card, then that location of the decimal will override the location specified by the "F" entry designation in the FØRMAT statement. For example, if the number 52.86 is to be read using an F10.4 designation (indicating card columns 1 through 10) and without the decimal punched, then to satisfy the FØRMAT statement, the numbers 5286 should be punched in card columns 5 through 8. Why? However, if the decimal is punched to separate the 2 and 8, 52.86 could be punched in card columns 1 through 5, 2 through 6, 3 through 7, 4 through 8, 5 through 9, or 6 through 10. Punched in any of these positions, the correct value would be assigned, provided the decimal is punched.

Since the "F" entry designation is often inadvertently misused by beginning programmers, the above will be reiterated. When using an "F" FØRMAT entry designation on input, the value to be assigned must be contained in the field width indicated (for F10.4, ten consecutive columns). If the decimal appears in the field, then the value appearing in the field is the value assigned. If no decimal appears in the field, then the value assigned is adjusted to conform to the "F" entry designation. In the above example, if 5286 was punched on a data card in columns 7 through 10, then the value read would be 0.5286. Contrast this to 52.86 punched in columns 6 through 10, which would result in a value read of 52.86. To avoid confusion, it is suggested that, for scientific or engineering problems, data should be prepared with the decimal punched in the exact location intended. The most important exception to this would be for situations in which there may be large quantities of data and one does not want to take the time to punch decimal points or to use up space on a card for them.

An example of a READ/FØRMAT combination of statements is as follows:

    READ(5,10)X,Y,J
10 FØRMAT(F10.2,F8.0,I6)

When this READ statement is executed, one data card will be read by the computer. This particular READ statement indicates that values are to be read for three variables — X, Y, and J. The designation F10.2 in the FØRMAT statement is associated with the variable X and indicates that the value of X will be contained within the first 10 columns on the data card. Two digits to the right of the decimal will be anticipated (but not mandatory if the decimal is punched). The designation F8.0 in the FØRMAT statement is associated with the variable Y and indicates that the value of Y will be contained in the next 8 columns on the same data card. No digits to the right of the decimal will be anticipated. The designation I6 in the FØRMAT statement is associated with the variable J and indicates that the value of J will be contained within the next 6 columns on the same data card. Thus if the values of X, Y, and J to be read are 27.2, 14., and 18, respectively, the data card would be arranged as follows:

Card Column

1	2	3	4	5	6	7	8	9	10	11	12	13	14	15	16	17	18	19	20	21	22	23	24	25
2	7	.	2	0									1	4	.							1	8	

As explained previously, the location of values for X and Y could vary each within its field — but not the location of J's value. Note there is no problem of carriage control as with the WRITE statement.

Upon execution of this particular READ statement, the numbers would be read from the data card and assigned to the variables named in accordance with the FØRMAT statement. Thus after execution, the value of 27.20 would be given to the variable X, the value of 14. would be given to the variable Y, and the value of 18 would be given to the variable J. The variables would retain these values unless they were changed through subsequent execution.

Note also that the values on the data cards determine the values of variables X, Y, and J. Therefore, the program itself does not have to be compiled more than once, even though several sets of values of X, Y, and J may be used on several "runs" of the program.

READ statements occur in the Fortran program, but data cards do not (data cards are not Fortran). The data cards for a program are grouped together in the order in which they are read and placed in a deck (the data deck) following the end of the program. Unlike statements in the Fortran program, which are limited to columns 7 through 72, data cards can use every column on the card (columns 1 through 80).

Each time a READ statement is executed in a program (referencing the card reader), there must be *at least* one data card in the deck to be read. For example, if there are ten READ statements to be executed in a program, there should be at least ten data cards. More than ten cards could be required depending on the length of the READ lists and the composition of the associated FØRMAT statements. Additionally, one READ statement can be executed any number of times depending on the statement's location in the logical flow of execution in the entire program. Consequently each time a READ statement is executed, it will require at least one new data card. Each time a READ is executed, all variables in the READ list can be assigned new values. Naturally, it is the programmer's responsibility to recognize the order of execution of the READ statements and to provide the necessary data cards in the correct order.

To illustrate the use of the READ statement, let's examine the following problem. Suppose one desired to find the perimeter of five different rectangles. To solve for the perimeters in a Fortran program, the length and the width of each rectangle would have to be introduced into the program, the perimeter calculated for each rectangle, and the perimeters (along with the associated dimensions) would be printed. Below is a list of the dimensions of the five rectangles:

Rectangle Number	Length(centimeters)	Width(centimeters)
1	5.0	4.0
2	6.6	3.5
3	4.8	2.0
4	7.9	5.2
5	6.0	1.4

The introduction of these values could be accomplished with the following READ statement:

READ(5,20)NUMBER,XLENG,WIDTH
20 FØRMAT(I2,2F4.1)

The data card required for the input of the information for the first rectangle would be:

Card Column 1 2 3 4 5 6 7 8 9 10 11 12 13 14 15 16 17 18 19 20
Data   1   5 . 0   4 . 0

When the above READ statement is executed and the above data card is read, the values of the three variables will be stored for use in computing the perimeter of rectangle number 1 and for printing the results. The same procedure would be followed for the four remaining rectangles. The total number of data cards required in this example would be five. (The sequence of execution of the statements in this example would require transfer back to the READ statement to consider all five rectangles. This concept will be the subject of Chap. 5.)

3-4   FREE FORMAT INPUT/OUTPUT

Standard Fortran (ANSI X3.9-1978) does not contain format-free or free format input/output. However, several versions of Fortran do allow input and output in this simplified manner. If problems being solved with Fortran programs require headings, labels, specific location of data, or involve complex number or character data, then the programmer will wish to consider using the standard formatted input/output covered in Sec. 3-1 through Sec. 3-3. However, if the computer system uses a version of Fortran with free format input/output, a programmer may consider it more desirable for short, less formal programs.

The free format input is usually of the following general form:

READ,list

where list is again a set of variable names separated by commas. Data cards must be included in the data deck and contain enough values to assign to all elements in the READ list. The values are punched on the data cards and must be separated by a delimiter — usually either one or more blank spaces or a comma. If blank spaces are used as delimiters, then one data card may contain one value or many values as desired by the programmer. When the READ statement is executed, the computer will read as many data cards as necessary to satisfy the READ list. Real constants may be expressed in decimal form or in exponent form.

Suppose that it was desired to introduce the following values into a program:

BETA=2.75
IØTA=3
GAMMA=.00418

This could be done using free format READ as follows:

READ,BETA,IØTA,GAMMA

The accompanying data card could be:

Card Column *1 2 3 4 5 6 7 8 9 10 11 12 13 14 15 16 17 18 19 20*
Data   **2 . 7 5 , 3 , . 4 1 8 E - 0 2**

Notice the commas in card columns 5 and 7. These could be replaced by blanks for some compilers. Also, the real constant .00418 is expressed here in exponent form. Obviously one advantage to this form of input is the saving of card columns (for example, in some previous examples the FØRMAT designations used had to allow for the largest values that variables could assume). In free format input, the values on the data cards are completely independent of FØRMAT designations and values of all sizes are simply separated by commas.

The free format output statement is the PRINT statement. Its general form is:

PRINT,list

The list is the set of variable names whose values are to be presented as output. Again, these variables must be separated by commas. The values indicated will be printed with enough spaces separating each one so as to insure legibility. Integer values will be printed as before — without decimals; however, real values will be printed as a decimal number followed by an exponent.

Returning to the last example, if one wished now to print the values of the three variables that were introduced, this could be accomplished by the following:

PRINT,BETA,IØTA,GAMMA

The output would appear as:

.275E 01   3   .418E-02

This would appear on the next line of output. Thus the carriage control is automatically the same as using a blank as the first character in a FØRMAT statement for formatted output. Extra lines would be automatically used to print all of the values in the PRINT list.

3-5 INPUT/OUTPUT WITH TERMINALS

Almost all of the material covered thus far has been limited to input via punched cards and the card reader, and output on the high-speed line printer and the standard 11 in. by 14-7/8 in. print paper. If a programmer wishes to use a terminal to submit input and/or to receive output, this is easily done; however, there are many considerations. The terminal itself can vary even within one remote facility of one computer system. There may be "hard-copy" terminals such as a teletype or printer terminals (see Chap. 1) or there may be CRT display terminals (which are excellent for rapid debugging of programs). Often a terminal allows only 72 characters per input or output record, but some terminals have larger record sizes.

Since there is a variety of terminals and Fortran compilers on different computer systems, an individual programmer desiring to use a terminal should investigate the interactive programming available locally. Usually classes or at least programmer aids are available for acquainting a programmer with the requirements of a specific computer center. Thus detailed coverage of terminal input/output is beyond the scope of any general programming text.

3-6 SUMMARY

This chapter has presented only the essentials of input/output. It is hoped that the reader will now be aware of the niceties of introducing and extracting data via a Fortran program. The problems that follow will reinforce this understanding and should be attempted to test the reader's full comprehension.

In later chapters, some extensions of these topics will be described. Certainly, the topics introduced in this chapter are sufficient for most applications. The in-depth study of a compiler reference manual (available from a computer system manufacturer) will provide the ultimate in input/output background.

3-7 PROBLEMS

3-1 Give the Fortran coding necessary to have your name printed at the top of the next page of output.

For Problems 3-2 through 3-9, indicate all that is wrong, if anything, with each of the statements or groups of statements.

3-2   READ(5,100),A,B,

3-3   FØRMAT(' ',F10.2)

3-4   WRITE,A,B

3-5   400 READ(5,400)A,B

3-6   WRITE(6,150)X,Y
        150 FØRMAT('1',2I6)

3-7   88 FØRMAT(10(8X,F12.3))

3-8   62 FØRMAT(1X,5F4.2,T15,I6)

3-9   READ(5,900)I,J
        900 FØRMAT(I6,F6.0)

Given the following illustrations of data cards, work Problems 3-10 through 3-13.

```
Card Column  1 2 3 4 5 6 7 8 9 10 11 12 13 14  . . .
Data Card#1  6 7 . 3     3 1 . 5  2
Data Card#2      7 3 4 5 6 2 1  7
Data Card#3  9 9     - 3 4
Data Card#4  2 9 . 0 3 5 8 1  1
```

3-10   What would the value of A be if the following was executed and card
#1 is used?
READ(5,10)A
10 FØRMAT(F5.2)

3-11   Same as Problem 3-10, except use card #2.

3-12   What would the value of all variables be upon executing the following (begin with data card #1)?
READ(5,435)XJ,Ø,Y,XM,A,T,S
435 FØRMAT(3F4.1)

3-13   Repeat Problem 3-12 for the following:
READ(5,1000)R,S,T,U,V,W
1000 FØRMAT(F6.0/F3.2,2X,F3.1/2X,2F3.0/F7.4)

3-14   Given the following lines of output, determine the FØRMAT statement necessary to produce the lines indicated if the output statement is: WRITE(6,50)DIST

Printed Column 1 2 3 4 5 6 7 8 9 10 11 12
Print Line #1   **D I S T A N C E**
Print Line #2   **F T .**
Print Line #3
Print Line #4   **7 8 3 . 5**

3-15   Consider Problem 3-14 again but modify the FØRMAT statement to
convey the same output information on one print line only.

3-16   Same as Problem 3-15 but use two print lines.

3-17   Give the Fortran coding necessary to "read" values for variables
ABLE and BAKER from columns 10 through 16 and columns 19
through 22, respectively, of a data card.

3-18   Give the coding required to "read" values for CHARLY and DELTA
using free format input.

3-19   Show the composition of the data card necessary for Problem 3-18 if
the value of variable CHARLY is 210.67 and the value of variable
DELTA is .000000126.

In Problems 3-20 through 3-22, give the resulting output (include all
blanks, denoted by "b").

3-20   A=21675.3
WRITE(6,95)A
95 FØRMAT('1',E15.5)
.
.
.

3-21   DATA BUM/4.56/
             WRITE(6,15)BUM
       15 FØRMAT(' THE CONSTANT BUM ='//F10.2)
             .
             .
             .
             .

3-22   H=11.5
             J=5
             Y=.0712001
             WRITE(6,940)H,J
     940 FØRMAT('1H = '/F6.2/'J = '/1X,I4/'Y =')
             PRINT,Y
             .
             .
             .

4
The Fortran Program

4-1 INTRODUCTION

A Fortran program consists of a series of Fortran statements in a specified order. The order is, of course, established by the programmer to carry out a desired sequence of computations.

It is difficult to explain in words how to write a computer program; this is probably best learned by observing example programs and by individual practice in writing other programs. The best procedure the authors have found to explain how to write a program is as follows:

(1) Look at the problem and think of the steps you would follow in solving the problem by hand or by pocket calculator.
(2) Prepare a flowchart (see Chap. 1) to show how these steps interrelate.
(3) Referring to the flowchart, transform the steps into Fortran statements.

The general idea behind the writing of the program is to establish a sequence of computations that can be repeated for different purposes.

4-2 CODING REQUIREMENTS

Normally, a program is written initially on a "coding sheet," with each Fortran statement on a separate line. While it is possible to write a program on a plain piece of paper, the use of a coding sheet is recommended. As shown in Fig. 4-1, a coding sheet has ruled and labeled lines and columns. As will be seen subsequently, certain items must appear in certain columns, and the use of a coding sheet should certainly be used if one person is writing a program and another will do the keypunching.

Further reference to Fig. 4-1 should facilitate the explanation as to which columns are used for what purposes. To begin with, the Fortran statement itself must be placed within columns 7 through 72. It is not necessary that the statement begin in column 7; it may

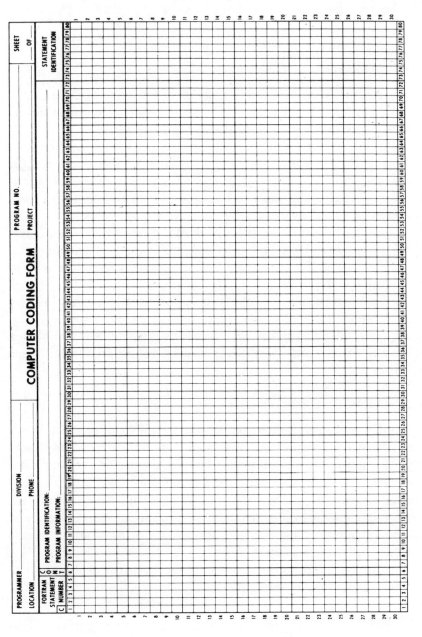

Figure 4-1. Sample Computer Coding Form

begin in column 7 or in any column to the right of column 7. In writing statements, blanks may be left between numbers, variables, and symbols as desired by the programmer to make it easier to read.

Columns 1 through 5 are reserved for a statement label, which is used to identify or refer to a particular statement. A statement label consists of any positive integer less than 100000. It is permissible to give a statement number to every Fortran statement; however, this is generally not desirable. The same statement number may not be used more than once in a given program. Normally, statement numbers are assigned only when necessary. As indicated in Chap. 3, every FØRMAT statement must have a statement number. Other statements may or may not require statement numbers, depending on the particular program. The order in which statements are numbered is arbitrary. They may be numbered consecutively or randomly.

If a particular statement is too long to be contained within columns 7 through 72 on one line, it may be continued on one or more succeeding lines by placing any nonzero character in column 6 of the second and succeeding lines. The statement is then continued on the second and succeeding lines within columns 7 through 72. If column 6 is not used in this manner to indicate a continued statement, it should be left blank.

Columns 73 through 80 are not used in writing Fortran statements. Inasmuch as these columns are ignored by the Fortran compiler, they can be used by the programmer to identify each line, to sequence number the deck, or otherwise, if desired.

In writing programs, it is helpful to include notes within the body of the program to explain what the program is doing at that location. This can be done by use of "comments." One or more comments may be placed anywhere in a program by placing a "C" in column 1. If a "C" appears in column 1, the remainder of the line may contain any comments desired. Comments will be ignored when the program is compiled except that the entire contents of the lines will be printed out along with the program in the locations where the comments appear. Liberal use of comments can greatly help anyone who later tries to understand what the programmer had in mind in composing the program.

4-3 PROGRAM DEVELOPMENT

The Fortran statements described in the two preceding sections comprise what is called the "source program." It is the program written in Fortran by the programmer to solve a particular problem. These statements (the source program) are usually punched on cards, with each line on the coding sheet being punched on a separate card. An example of a punched card is given in Fig. 4-2. The resulting card deck is fed into a card reader, which translates the punched information (i.e., the holes punched into the cards) into a form that the computer can handle internally.

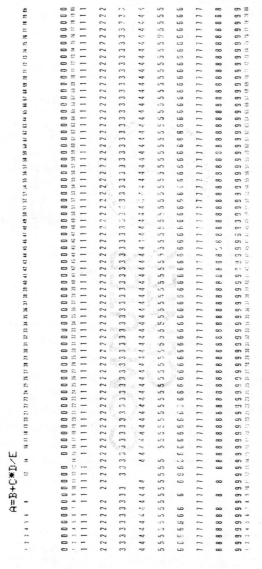

Figure 4-2. Example of a Punched Card

The Fortran statements of the source program are translated by a Fortran compiler program into a more basic language (machine language). This process is called the "compilation" of the program. The program now in machine language is called the "object program." It is this program that is subsequently executed to perform the computations specified by the programmer in the source program and to obtain the required results. This is the "execution" of the program.

A complete set of cards normally required to run a program consists of (1) a source program (described above), (2) data cards, if required for the particular program (Chap. 3), and (3) job control cards. Job control cards are used to convey certain information not related to the source program, such as programmer's name, account number, what to do with the source program and data, etc. Specific job control cards required are highly variable from one computer system to another; hence it would be futile to try to give any specific information on them here. One must, of course, learn the control card requirements for the particular computer system being used.

A typical setup of the complete deck of cards required to run a program would consist of some control cards, followed by the (Fortran) source program, followed by the data cards, if required. One or more control cards may be required between the source program and the data cards and/or after the data cards.

4-4 EXAMPLE PROGRAMS

The time has now come to begin writing programs. An extremely simple problem will be considered first. After reviewing the program written for this problem, the reader is urged to punch this program, supply the necessary control cards, and run the program in order to learn the run procedure. (If instead a terminal is being used, the information would be entered via the terminal console.)

EXAMPLE 4-1

Write a computer program that will compute the area (in hectares) of a rectangular parcel of property that is 816.2 m long and 655.4 m wide.

Solution:

A flowchart for solving this problem is given in Fig. 4-3. A

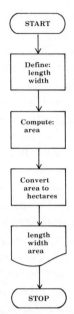

Figure 4-3.   Flow Chart for Example 4-1

program for solving this problem is given below.

```
C
CØMMENT--ESTABLISH VALUES ØF LENGTH AND WIDTH
C
        XL=816.2
        W=655.4
C
CØMMENT--CØMPUTE AREA
C
        AREA=XL*W
C
CØMMENT--CØNVERT AREA TØ HECTARES
C
        AREA=AREA/10000.
C
CØMMENT--WRITE ØUT RESULTS
C
        WRITE(6,5)XL,W,AREA
      5 FØRMAT('1IF LENGTH =',F6.1,' M AND WIDTH =',
       *F6.1,' M, AREA =',F6.2,' HECTARES.')
        STØP
        END
```

Example 4-1 presents a very simple programming example, but it is worthy of considerable elaboration at this point. The first two statements (not counting the comment card) in the program establish (by means of arithmetic assignment statements) the given values of the length and of the width, and the third statement computes the value of AREA as the product of the length and the width. The fourth statement converts the area just determined into hectares by dividing by the number of square meters in a hectare. With the area now determined in hectares, the next step is to write out the answer; this is accomplished by the WRITE statement (fifth statement) and associated FØRMAT statement (sixth statement). Note that the FØRMAT statement is too long to fit within columns 7 through 72 and is therefore continued on the next line by placing an asterisk (any letter, digit other than zero, or symbol could have been used) in column 6 on the second line.

The output from the program written in Example 4-1 would be printed on the first line of a new page as follows:

IF LENGTH = 816.2 M AND WIDTH = 655.4 M, AREA = 53.49 HECTARES.

Inasmuch as the "answer" to the problem posed in Example 4-1 is simply the value of the area of the rectangle, one might wonder why the values of the length and the width were also written. The reason is that it is good practice to write out all pertinent data so that the output will be more or less self-explanatory and will stand on its own. If, for example, only the area had been written, an observer would not know what the area represented, without referring back to the program. Also, as will be related in the next chapter, the same program may be used to solve many different problems by varying the input data, resulting in many different answers (values of the area in Example 4-1). To have a large number of pages of output each containing only a value of area would be almost useless, since it would not easily be known what input data gave each area. If, however, each page of output listed the input data along with the associated value of the area (as in Example 4-1), the results would be quite useful. In summary, output should include all pertinent data arranged in a neat, orderly form. Note also that the output from Example 4-1 includes units on the output data (i.e., m and hectares in this case).

The order in which statements are listed in a program is of importance, as statements are executed sequentially in the order they appear unless directed otherwise. (Chapter 5 will show how to alter the sequential order of execution.) In Example 4-1 the first statement executed is, of course, the one that sets XL equal to 816.2, and the second is the one that sets W equal to 655.4. The third statement executed is the one that computes the area by multiplying XL by W. It is absolutely necessary that this statement appear after the first two so that the values of XL and W are assigned prior to using them on the right side of the arithmetic assignment statement to compute the value of AREA. (If the value of XL and/or W had not been assigned prior to using them on the right side of the arithmetic assignment statement, a value of zero or any other number previously stored in that particular computer memory location might have been substituted, an error message might have been printed, or some other action might have been taken, depending on the particular computer system.) The next step executed is the one that converts the area to hectares. It must occur after the preceding statement so that the value of AREA in square meters is known prior to using it on the right side of the arithmetic assignment statement to compute the value of AREA in hectares. The next step executed is the WRITE statement, and it is absolutely necessary that it appear after the first four so that values of XL, W, and AREA will be known when the WRITE statement is executed. (If the value of any variable in the list to be written out has not been assigned at execution time, a value of zero might be written out, an error message might be printed, or some other action might be taken, depending on the particular computer system.) Note that the value of AREA written is expressed in hectares. Although the value was computed in square meters in the third statement, that (the "square meter value") was wiped out when the fourth statement was executed. Thus the value assigned to AREA when the WRITE statement is executed is the "hectare value." If the fourth and fifth statements were interchanged, the value of AREA written would have been the "square meter value." These first five statements must appear in the order given, except that the first two could be interchanged without changing the results. The FØRMAT statement is not an executable statement; its placement after the WRITE statement is not a necessity. It may be placed anywhere in the program prior to the END statement.

The last two statements in the program written for Example 4-1 should appear in any program. The next to last statement (STØP) is an executable statement that means to cease execution of the program. Most often it appears in the next to last position, but it may be placed anywhere in the program at which termination of execution is desired. There may be more than one STØP statement in a program. The END statement is necessary to identify the last statement in the Fortran program.

The program written for the problem of Example 4-1 is not the only program that could be written for the given problem. Five people independently writing a program for the same problem would likely come up with five different programs, all of which could be correct. For example, the program of Example 4-1 could have been written using a READ statement and associated FØRMAT to input the values of XL and W rather than the arithmetic assignment statements used in the example program. In this case the first two statements could be replaced by the following:

    READ(5,9)XL,W
  9 FØRMAT(2F6.1)

This would, of course, require a data card that would be punched as shown below and placed after the source deck.

   Column   *1 2 3 4 5 6 7 8 9 10 11 12 13 14*----------
   Data   8 1 6 . 2   6 5 5 . 4

As another alternative, it would be possible to combine all of the first four statements of the program of Example 4-1 into a single statement as follows:

  AREA=816.2*655.4/10000.

While this is acceptable for this particular problem, it more or less defeats the purpose of programming. As will be related in Chap. 5, one major benefit of programming is to process large amounts of data, and this requires the use of variable names for the various input parameters (rather than expressing them all explicitly as in the statement above).

Two final, minor comments relate to the program written for Example 4-1. One is to note that the variable name XL (rather than L) was used for the length of the rectangle. This was done to make a real variable name for the length. The other item is to note the use of comment cards in this example problem. Their use in this program should make it more or less understandable to most anyone.

EXAMPLE 4-2

The Manning formula for computing the average velocity of water flow in a stream is

$$v = \frac{1.486}{n} R^{2/3} s^{1/2}$$

where v = velocity, in ft/sec

      n = roughness coefficient

      R = hydraulic radius, in ft

      s = slope of the stream (dimensionless)

(The hydraulic radius is equal to the cross section area of flow divided by its wetted perimeter. The wetted perimeter is the perimeter along the cross section that is in contact with the water. For a rectangular cross section, the hydraulic radius is equal to the product of the depth and width divided by the sum of the width plus twice the depth.) Suppose the roughness coefficient is 0.013, the width and depth of a rectangular cross section are 100 ft and 20 ft (respectively), and the slope is 0.0001. Write a computer program that will solve for the velocity.

Solution:

A flowchart for solving this problem is given in Fig. 4-4. A

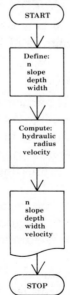

Figure 4-4. Flow Chart for Example 4-2

program for solving this problem is given below.

```
C
CØMMENT--ESTABLISH INPUT VALUES
C
        XN=.013
        SLØPE=.0001
        DEPTH=20.
        WIDTH=100.
C
CØMMENT--CØMPUTE HYDRAULIC RADIUS
C
        HYRAD=WIDTH*DEPTH/(WIDTH+2.*DEPTH)
C
CØMMENT--CØMPUTE VELØCITY
C
        V=1.486/XN*HYRAD**(2./3.)*SQRT(SLØPE)
C
CØMMENT--WRITE ØUT RESULTS
C
        WRITE(6,8)XN,SLØPE,DEPTH,WIDTH,V
      8 FØRMAT('1  RØUGHNESS CØEFF.  SLØPE'
       *'  DEPTH  WIDTH  VELOCITY'/
       *32X,'(FT)  (FT)  (FT/SEC)'/8X,F9.3,9X,
       *F6.4,F7.0,F9.0,F9.1)
        STØP
        END
```

After scrutinizing the program written in Example 4-1, the reader should be able to follow the program of Example 4-2 readily. This program requires the computation of an intermediate answer (HYRAD) prior to computing the final answer (V). The output from this program is presented somewhat differently (from Example 4-1) with answers beneath topical headings, as shown below:

RØUGHNESS CØEFF.	SLØPE	DEPTH	WIDTH	VELØCITY
		(FT)	(FT)	(FT/SEC)
0.013	0.0001	20.	100.	6.7

4-5 "DEBUGGING" THE PROGRAM

Source programs, described in the previous section, are punched and then "run" through the computer. The results printed by the computer will generally include a listing of the program as well as the answers.

Sometimes the programmer may find that answers are either missing or incorrect. *Missing* answers often result from illegal procedures such as two operation symbols placed together, incorrect punctuation, nonagreement between an output statement and associated FØRMAT, and so on. Often these kinds of errors are flagged by error messages on the program listing from the computer. *Incorrect* answers often result from incorrect logic by the programmer, incorrect statement sequencing, incorrect use of (or lack of use of) parentheses, incorrect use of mixed mode, or simple errors such as placing a plus sign in place of a minus sign, etc. In any event, the programmer should always verify his or her answers, and if they are incorrect or missing, he or she must carefully examine the program listing, make necessary corrections, and rerun the program. Sometimes this will require going through the program step by step and performing each computation (using a hand held calculator) just as the computer did in order to find the "bug" in the program. Frequently a program will have to be corrected and rerun many times before the program is perfected. This is known as "debugging" the program.

In summary, the first step in debugging a program is to eliminate syntax errors, the second step is to eliminate execution errors, and the third step is to verify accuracy.

4-6 PROBLEMS

4-1 A weir is an opening in a channel through and over which water flows. For the triangular weir shown in Fig. 4-5, the flow rate,

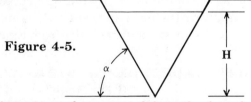

Figure 4-5.

q (ft³/sec), can be computed from the formula

$$q = 2.48 \ H^{2.5}/\tan \alpha$$

where H is measured in ft.

Write a program that will compute q if H is 3.3 ft and α is 50°.

4-2 Repeat Problem 4-1 for H equal to 4.1 ft and α equal to 45°.

4-3 Write a program that will use the equation given in Problem 4-1 to compute the value of H that would give a flow rate of 20 ft³/sec if α is 48°.

4-4 Repeat Problem 4-3 if q is 32 ft³/sec and α is 55°.

4-5 In an electrical circuit, resistors in parallel (as shown in Fig. 4-6)

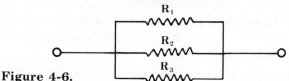

Figure 4-6.

can be replaced by a single resistor R as given by the formula

$$1/R = 1/R_1 + 1/R_2 + 1/R_3 + \dots$$

In this equation R_1, R_2, R_3, etc., are the respective resistors in parallel. All values of R are in units of ohms. Write a program that will compute and write out the replacement resistor R if R_1 is 30 ohms, R_2 is 40 ohms, and R_3 is 45 ohms.

4-6 The torque, T, in a solid shaft can be computed from the formula

$$T = 63{,}000 \ hp/R$$

where T = torque, in lb-in.
hp = horsepower transmitted by shaft
R = shaft rotation, in rpm

The required shaft diameter can be computed from the formula

$$d = 1.72 \ (T/s)^{1/3}$$

where d = shaft diameter, in in.
s = allowable stress in shaft, in lb/in.²

Write a program that will compute and write out the required shaft diameter if horsepower is 450, rotation is 4000 rpm, and allowable stress is 14,000 lb/in.².

4-7 If an object is accelerated at a constant rate, a (cm/sec²), for a length of time, t (sec), the displacement (i.e., distance travelled), s (cm), can be computed from the formula

$$s = v_0 t + (1/2) \ at^2$$

where v_0 is the initial velocity in cm/sec.

Write a program that will compute and write out the displacement for an initial velocity of 3.0 cm/sec, an acceleration of 2.5 cm/sec², and a time of 10.6 sec.

4-8 Alternating current power can be computed from the formula

$$P = EI \cos \phi$$

where P = power, in watts
       E = effective voltage, in volts
       I = effective current, in amps
       ϕ = phase angle, in degrees

Write a program that will compute and write out the power if E is 50 volts, I is 35 amps, and ϕ is 88°.

4-9   Using the formula given in Problem 4-8, write a program that will compute and write out the voltage required for a power of 66 watts, if I is 46 amps and ϕ is 85°.

4-10 The area of a triangle can be computed from the formula

$$A = \sqrt{s(s-a)(s-b)(s-c)}$$

where a, b, and c are the respective lengths of the three sides and s is half the sum of the lengths of the three sides.

Write a program that will compute and write out the area of a triangle with sides of 112.22 cm, 163.89 cm, and 169.90 cm.

5
Program Control

5-1 INTRODUCTION

In Chap. 4 a program was written (Example 4-2) to compute the average velocity (v) of water moving in a stream if the roughness coefficient (n), slope (s), depth (d), and width (w) are known. This simple program defined the value of the latter four parameters and then used these parameters to compute and write out the value of the velocity. The program then stopped.

While this is certainly a legitimate program, it is not a particularly useful one. If someone needed to solve for v, given the values of n, s, d, and w in the previous problem, it would certainly be easier to grab a modern handheld calculator, punch the numbers in, and read the answer than it would be to write a computer program (as the one in Chap. 4), punch it, and run it on a computer. Generally, it is not feasible to write a computer program to make just one computation such as this unless the computation is extremely complicated; and even then, the complicated computation could probably be handled easily with the modern calculator. Why, then, use a computer?

One answer to that question is that it is frequently convenient or even necessary to do computations of a repetitive nature, a task for which the computer is phenomenally successful. In order to make a computer do this, one must learn about program control and control statements. These are the topic of this chapter.

5-2 THE GØ TØ STATEMENT

Ordinarily, the statements in a Fortran program are executed sequentially in the order in which they appear in the program unless something is done to change the order. The simplest means of changing that order is by use of the unconditional GØ TØ statement.

The unconditional GØ TØ statement takes the form

GØ TØ n

where n is some statement number. The GØ TØ statement, like every other Fortran statement, must begin in column 7 or farther to the right. Whenever a GØ TØ statement appears in a program and is executed, the next statement executed is the one designated in the GØ TØ statement. Execution then continues sequentially *at the new location* until something is done to change the order. For example, in the skeleton program below, statements would be executed in the following order: 1,2,3,6,7,8,4,5,1,2,3,6,7,8,4,5,1, etc.

1 xxxx
2 xxxx
3 GØ TØ 6
4 xxxx
5 GØ TØ 1
6 xxxx
7 xxxx
8 GØ TØ 4

As a more practical example, let us modify the program written in Example 4-2 in Chap. 4, in which it was desired to compute the velocity for a given value of n, slope, depth, and width.

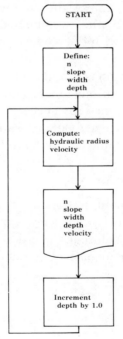

Figure 5-1. Flow Chart for Example 5-1

EXAMPLE 5-1

Modify the problem given in Example 4-2 to require that the velocity be computed for all values of depth beginning at 20 ft and incrementing by 1 ft. (Other data are to remain the same.)

SOLUTION:

The program written in Example 4-2 computes the desired velocity only for a depth of 20 ft. The program can be modified by incrementing the depth by 1 ft after the velocity has been computed for a depth of 20 ft and then causing the calculations to be executed again. The flow chart of Fig. 4-4 has been modified to reflect this change, as shown in Fig. 5-1. The specific modification of the program written in Example 4-2 can be accomplished by placing the following two statements before the STØP command.

> DEPTH=DEPTH+1.
> GØ TØ 200

It would then be necessary to give the statement number 200 to the fifth statement in the program. The modified program would be

```
CØMMENT--ESTABLISH INPUT VALUES
C
          XN=.013
          SLØPE=.0001
          DEPTH=20.
          WIDTH=100.
C
CØMMENT--CØMPUTE HYDRAULIC RADIUS
C
     200 HYRAD=WIDTH*DEPTH/(WIDTH+2.*DEPTH)
C
CØMMENT--CØMPUTE VELØCITY
C
          V=1.486/XN*HYRAD**(2./3.)*SQRT(SLØPE)
C
CØMMENT--WRITE ØUT RESULTS
C
          WRITE(6,8)XN,SLØPE,DEPTH,WIDTH,V
        8 FØRMAT('1   RØUGHNESS CØEFF.  SLØPE'
         *'  DEPTH   WIDTH   VELOCITY'/
         *32X,'(FT)   (FT)   (FT/SEC)'/8X,F9.3,9X,
         *F6.4,F7.0,F9.0,F9.1)
```

```
C
CØMMENT--INCREMENT DEPTH BY 1 FT
C
        DEPTH=DEPTH+1.
C
CØMMENT--RETURN TØ CØMPUTE VELØCITY FØR NEW
C       DEPTH
C
        GØ TØ 200
        STØP
        END
```

If the program above for Example 5-1 is executed, the program will run as before (in Example 4-2) through the WRITE statement for a depth of 20 ft. Instead of stopping as before, the statement after number 8 causes the value of DEPTH to be increased by 1 ft to 21 ft. The next statement then sends control to the newly numbered statement 200. At this point a new value of HYRAD will be computed, since the value of DEPTH on the right has been changed. The next statement computes a new value of V, since there is a new value of HYRAD on the right. The next statement then writes out values of the stated variables. The values of XN, SLØPE, and WIDTH will be the same as before, but there will, of course, be new values of DEPTH and V. The value of DEPTH will again be incremented by 1, giving a value of 22 ft. Control then returns to statement 200, and the program runs again for a depth of 22. And so on.

The program of Example 5-1 is "legal," but it does contain a couple of pitfalls (and should therefore not be executed in its present form). First, the program, as written, would continue indefinitely — running over and over — each time for a new value of DEPTH. Obviously, a program such as this would not be satisfactory, as it would, in theory, never stop (not at least until the value of DEPTH or one of the other variables became too large for the computer to handle). In reality, the program would likely be stopped eventually, either directly or indirectly, by the operator. The second pitfall concerns the fact that the output from this program would be written out with each line of output at the top of a separate page. (This is because of the "1" in the first record position, or carriage control, of the FØRMAT statement.) Clearly this would be undesirable from the standpoint of conservation of paper.

These pitfalls can be avoided by modifying the program to provide a natural means of stopping the program (such as stopping it when the value of DEPTH reaches some specified value) and to place each line of output directly below the previous one (rather than having each on a separate page). These modifications will be illustrated subsequently (Example 5-2), but it is first necessary to discuss "IF" statements.

5-3 IF STATEMENTS

"IF" statements are conditional, meaning that the next statement to be executed is dependent on the current evaluation of the IF statement. There are two types of IF statement — the "arithmetic IF statement" and the "logical IF statement."

The arithmetic IF statement takes the form

IF(exp)n,z,p

where n, z, and p are statement numbers. The parentheses must contain a Fortran expression. When an arithmetic IF statement is executed, the value of the expression within the parentheses is computed, and the next statement executed will be either n, z, or p, depending on the computed value of the expression. If the sign of the computed value of the expression is negative, the next statement executed will be "n"; if the sign is positive, the next statement executed will be "p"; and if the computed value of the expression is zero, the next statement executed will be "z". Execution then continues sequentially *at the new location* until something is done to change the order. It is possible for two of the statement numbers n, z, and p to be the same number.

The logical IF statement takes the form

IF(exp)statement

With the logical IF, the parentheses must contain a "logical" expression (having only values of true or false), as opposed to an arithmetic expression in the arithmetic IF statement. The logical expression takes the general form "something is greater than (or less than, or equal to, etc.) something else." The indication "greater than" is made by using the abbreviation ".GT.". Suppose the desired condition is "the variable A greater than 100.". This could be indicated by the logical expression

A.GT.100.

A list of possible expressions is as follows:

Expression	*Meaning*
A.GT.100.	A greater than 100.
A.GE.100.	A greater than or equal to 100.
A.LT.100.	A less than 100.
A.LE.100.	A less than or equal to 100.
A.EQ.100.	A equal to 100.
A.NE.100.	A not equal to 100.

The statement to the right of the parentheses in a logical IF statement may be an arithmetic statement, an input/output statement, an unconditional GØ TØ statement, or STØP. Thus some sample logical IF statements are

IF(B.LT.26.4)GØ TØ 6
IF((A+X).NE.(B/C))A=B+C
IF(RST.GE..1)WRITE(6,66)RST

When a logical IF statement is executed, the expression within the parentheses is evaluated. If the value of the expression is "true" at that instant, then the statement to the right of the parentheses is executed next. The statement immediately following the logical IF statement is executed next unless the statement to the right of the parentheses is an unconditional GØ TØ. In that case the next statement executed is the one indicated by the GØ TØ. If the value of the expression within the parentheses is "not true" at that instant, then the statement to the right of the parentheses is ignored and the statement following the logical IF is executed next.

Sometimes it is desirable to have two or more expressions within the parentheses in a logical IF statement. There are several ways this can be done. One is to use ".AND." between two expressions. In this case, the statement to the right of the parentheses in the IF statement will be executed only if *both* expressions are true. Another is to use ".OR." between two expressions. In this case, the statement to the right of the parentheses will be executed if *either* expression is true. Another situation is to use ".NOT." before an expression. Here the statement to the right of the parentheses will be executed only if the expression is *not* true.

An example of a logical IF statement is

IF(G.LT.120..AND.B.GT.0.)GØ TØ 6

In this case, the statement GØ TØ 6 would be executed *only if both* G is less than 120. *and* B is greater than zero.

With IF statements having been presented, we can now modify the program of Example 5-1 to avoid the pitfalls noted at the end of Sec. 5-2.

EXAMPLE 5-2

Modify the program written for Example 5-1 so that the velocity will be computed for all values of DEPTH in the range of 20 ft to 50 ft in increments of 1 ft. (Other data are to remain the same.)

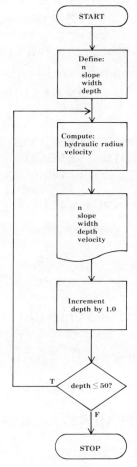

Figure 5-2. Flow Chart for Example 5-2

SOLUTION:

The program written in Example 5-1 can be modified simply by replacing the statement

GØ TØ 200

by the logical IF statement

   IF(DEPTH.LE.50.)GØ TØ 200

In order to avoid having each line of output on a separate page, it is necessary to place a WRITE statement with FØRMAT statement at the beginning of the program for the purpose of writing out the column headings at the top of a page. By doing this and by removing the "headings" from the FØRMAT (statement number 8), column headings are written out only once (at the top of a page) and the answers are written out on separate lines below. Figure 5-2 gives the flow chart for this modified program.

The complete (modified) program would be

```
CØMMENT--WRITE ØUT CØLUMN HEADINGS
C
         WRITE(6,88)
      88 FØRMAT('1    RØUGHNESS CØEFF.   SLØPE'
        *'  DEPTH   WIDTH   VELOCITY'/
        *32X,'(FT)    (FT)   (FT/SEC)')
C
CØMMENT--ESTABLISH INPUT VALUES
C
         XN=.013
         SLØPE=.0001
         DEPTH=20.
         WIDTH=100.
C
CØMMENT--CØMPUTE HYDRAULIC RADIUS
C
     200 HYRAD=WIDTH*DEPTH/(WIDTH+2.*DEPTH)
C
CØMMENT--CØMPUTE VELØCITY
C
         V=1.486/XN*HYRAD**(2./3.)*SQRT(SLØPE)
C
CØMMENT--WRITE ØUT RESULTS
C
         WRITE(6,8)XN,SLØPE,DEPTH,WIDTH,V
       8 FØRMAT(8X,F9.3,9X,F6.4,F7.0,F9.0,F9.1)
C
CØMMENT--INCREMENT DEPTH BY 1 FT
C
         DEPTH=DEPTH+1.
```

```
C
CØMMENT--IF DEPTH IS LESS THAN ØR EQUAL TØ 50,
C          RETURN TØ CØMPUTE VELØCITY FOR NEW DEPTH
C
          IF(DEPTH.LE.50.)GØ TØ 200
          STØP
          END
```

The output from the program written for Example 5-2 would be as follows:

ROUGHNESS COEFF.	SLOPE	DEPTH (FT)	WIDTH (FT)	VELOCITY (FT/SEC)
0.013	0.0001	20.	100.	6.7
0.013	0.0001	21.	100.	6.9
0.013	0.0001	22.	100.	7.0
0.013	0.0001	23.	100.	7.2
0.013	0.0001	24.	100.	7.3
0.013	0.0001	25.	100.	7.5
0.013	0.0001	26.	100.	7.6
0.013	0.0001	27.	100.	7.7
0.013	0.0001	28.	100.	7.8
0.013	0.0001	29.	100.	8.0
0.013	0.0001	30.	100.	8.1
0.013	0.0001	31.	100.	8.2
0.013	0.0001	32.	100.	8.3
0.013	0.0001	33.	100.	8.4
0.013	0.0001	34.	100.	8.5
0.013	0.0001	35.	100.	8.6
0.013	0.0001	36.	100.	8.7
0.013	0.0001	37.	100.	8.8
0.013	0.0001	38.	100.	8.9
0.013	0.0001	39.	100.	9.0
0.013	0.0001	40.	100.	9.0
0.013	0.0001	41.	100.	9.1
0.013	0.0001	42.	100.	9.2
0.013	0.0001	43.	100.	9.3
0.013	0.0001	44.	100.	9.4
0.013	0.0001	45.	100.	9.4
0.013	0.0001	46.	100.	9.5
0.013	0.0001	47.	100.	9.6
0.013	0.0001	48.	100.	9.6
0.013	0.0001	49.	100.	9.7
0.013	0.0001	50.	100.	9.8

Examination of the program written for Example 5-2 reveals that the very first statement executed causes what turns out to be column headings to be written out at the top of a page. (They are written at the top of a page because the carriage control is "1".) Execution then proceeds through the statement after statement number 8 in the same manner as in the program of Example 5-1. After the DEPTH has been incremented by 1 in this statement, it is necessary to determine whether or not the (new) value of DEPTH is greater than 50. If it is, the objective of the program has been achieved and the program may be terminated. If the (new) value of DEPTH is not greater than 50., it would be necessary to send control to statement number 200 to compute a new value of HYRAD, then a new value of V, and then to write out again the values of the variables listed in the WRITE statement. The value of DEPTH will be incremented by 1 again, and the (new) value of DEPTH checked again in the IF statement to see if the (new) value is greater than 50. The reader should verify that this program does operate in the manner indicated, does write out the output as indicated, and does terminate when the value of DEPTH exceeds 50.

This program could have been written using an arithmetic IF statement instead of the logical IF statement that was used. An appropriate arithmetic IF statement would be

IF(DEPTH-50.5)200,200,201

If this statement is used, it would be necessary to label the STØP statement as 201. If these modifications are made, the resulting program would be equivalent to the one given in Example 5-2. The reader should verify this.

One additional comment about the program of Example 5-2 is in order. Note that the program as written causes column headings to be written out at the top of a page and then the numerical answers are written out on separate lines below the column headings. The column headings are written out only one time because the WRITE statement that writes out the headings is executed only one time. Beginning programmers sometimes make the mistake of placing the WRITE statement to write out the headings "inside the loop" (i.e., after statement number 200 is this example) with the result that headings are written out at the top of a new page prior to each line of (numerical) output. This should be avoided unless, of course, alternating headings and (numerical) output are desired.

The program written for Example 5-2 is certainly more useful than the one written for Example 4-2, but it is limited by the fact that only one parameter is allowed to vary and it by a specified amount each time. It would be nice if programs of a repetitive nature could be run such that more than one parameter could vary and they by differing amounts. This can be easily and effectively done by incorporating the READ statement in the previous example, as shown in Example 5-3.

EXAMPLE 5-3
Suppose it is desired to compute the velocity for the following five different combinations of values of n, slope, depth, and width:

n	slope	depth (feet)	width (feet)
.013	.0001	20.	100.
.020	.0002	30.	200.
.025	.0003	80.	80.
.015	.0001	50.	100.
.018	.0003	60.	200.

SOLUTION:
In this case, the first set of values can be established with the use of the following READ statement:

READ(5,20)XN,SLØPE,DEPTH,WIDTH
20 FØRMAT(F5.3,F5.4,2F5.0)

The data card would be as follows:

column	1	2	3	4	5	6	7	8	9	10	11	12	13	14	15	16	17	18	19	20
data		.	0	1	3	.	0	0	0	1			2	0	.		1	0	0	.

(The FØRMAT entries above could have been 4F5.0, since the decimals for the four values are actually punched on the data card.)

When this READ statement is executed and the above data card is "read", the values of the variables named will be stored. This READ statement does, in effect, exactly the same thing that the first four statements in the previous example programs do. The remainder of the program would be modified so that, after the velocity is determined and written out for the first set of data, the program would return and read the next data card and determine and write out the velocity for the next set of data. It would be necessary to set up the program so that it would run five times. A flow chart for the modified program is given in Fig. 5-3. The complete program would be

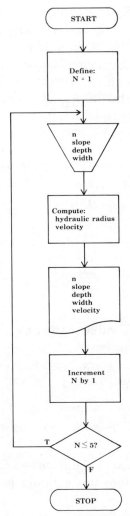

Figure 5-3.   Flow Chart for Example 5-3

CØMMENT--WRITE ØUT CØLUMN HEADINGS
C
      WRITE(6,88)
   88 FØRMAT('1   RØUGHNESS CØEFF. SLØPE'
    *' DEPTH   WIDTH   VELØCITY'/
    *32X,'(FT)   (FT) (FT/SEC)')
C
CØMMENT--SET CØUNTER EQUAL TØ 1
C
      N=1

```
C
CØMMENT--READ INPUT DATA
C
    200 READ(5,20)XN,SLØPE,DEPTH,WIDTH
     20 FØRMAT(F5.3,F5.4,2F5.0)
C
CØMMENT--CØMPUTE HYDRAULIC RADIUS
C
        HYRAD=WIDTH*DEPTH/(WIDTH+2.*DEPTH)
C
CØMMENT--CØMPUTE VELØCITY
C
        V=1.486/XN*HYRAD**(2./3.)*SQRT(SLØPE)
C
CØMMENT--WRITE ØUT RESULTS
C
        WRITE(6,8)XN,SLØPE,DEPTH,WIDTH,V
      8 FØRMAT(8X,F9.3,9X,F6.4,F7.0,F9.0,F9.1)
C
CØMMENT--INCREMENT CØUNTER BY 1
C
        N=N+1
C
CØMMENT--IF CØUNTER IS LESS THAN ØR EQUAL TØ 5,
C          RETURN TØ READ NEXT DATA CARD
C
        IF(N.LE.5)GØ TØ 200
        STØP
        END
```

The data cards would be punched as follows:

column	1	2	3	4	5	6	7	8	9	10	11	12	13	14	15	16	17	18	19	20
card 1	.	0	1	3	.	0	0	0	1				2	0	.		1	0	0	.
card 2	.	0	2	0	.	0	0	0	2				3	0	.		2	0	0	.
card 3	.	0	2	5	.	0	0	0	3				8	0	.			8	0	.
card 4	.	0	1	5	.	0	0	0	1				5	0	.		1	0	0	.
card 5	.	0	1	8	.	0	0	0	3				6	0	.		2	0	0	.

The output from the program written for Example 5-3 would be as follows:

ROUGHNESS COEFF.	SLOPE	DEPTH (FT)	WIDTH (FT)	VELOCITY (FT/SEC)
0.013	0.0001	20.	100.	6.7
0.020	0.0002	30.	200.	8.5
0.025	0.0003	80.	80.	9.2
0.015	0.0001	50.	100.	8.5
0.018	0.0003	60.	200.	16.0

The counter (N) in the program above causes the program to loop back five times. Each time new values of n, slope, depth, and width are read, a corresponding value of velocity is computed, and results are written out.

It would be desirable to make the program a little more flexible so that the program could be run for any desired number of data cards without having to change the program. This could be accomplished by placing a data card at the beginning of the data deck that tells how many data cards follow. This code number (an integer) would be read initially and, in the IF statement, the value of the counter N would be compared against the code number to see if the program has run the required number of times.

Another method to make the program more flexible so that the program could be run for any desired number of data cards without having to change the program is to place a blank data card at the end of the deck. When this card is routinely read, the values of XN, SLØPE, DEPTH, and WIDTH would all be zero. This is because whenever a variable is read under an F or I FØRMAT from a data card containing all blanks where it is indicated (by the FØRMAT) that the value of the variable is to appear, the value of the variable is taken to be zero by the computer. An IF statement can then be placed after the READ statement to determine when the last card (i.e., the blank card) has been read and to stop the program at that time. This method has the advantage over the last method of not requiring that the exact number of data cards be known before the program is run.

It will be left as an exercise for the reader to modify the program of Example 5-3 by each of the methods above to make it more flexible so that the program can be run for any desired number of data cards without having to change the program itself.

5-4 BLOCK-IF

Standard Fortran (ANSI X3.9-1978) includes a means of control referred to as "block-IF." This is promulgated as a feature of

"Structured Fortran." The reader is cautioned that the block-IF feature is not available on all Fortran compilers.

Block-IF may take the form

IF(exp)THEN
> st_1
> st_2
> st_3
> .
> .
> .
> **st_n**
END IF

With this block-IF structure, the parentheses must contain a logical expression. Upon execution, the expression within the parentheses is examined. If the expression is "true" at that instant, then the statements that follow (designated st_1, st_2, st_3, ... st_n) are executed through the END IF statement and normal execution continues with the next statement after the END IF. If the expression within the parentheses is "not true" at that instant, then the next statement executed will be the one immediately after the END IF, and the intervening statements will be ignored.

One will note that this IF-THEN structure is similar to a logical IF. The main difference is that the logical IF allows only one statement to be executed when the expression within the parentheses is true while the IF-THEN allows more than one statement to be executed when the expression is true.

Another form of block-IF is

IF(exp)THEN
> st_1
> st_2
> st_3
> .
> .
> .
> **st_n**
ELSE
> sf_1
> sf_2
> sf_3

.
.
.

$$sf_n$$
END IF

With this block-IF structure, the parentheses must again contain a
logical expression. Upon execution, the expression is examined. If
the condition is "true" at that instant, then the statements that
follow down to the ELSE statement (designated st_1, st_2, st_3, ...st_n)
are executed and normal execution continues with the next
statement after the END IF. If the expression within the parentheses is "not true" at that instant, then the statements between the
ELSE and the END IF (designated sf_1, sf_2, sf_3, ... sf_n) are executed
next and normal execution continues with the next statement after
the END IF.

Two admonitions with regard to the IF-THEN structure are
worth noting here. First, every IF-THEN statement must be
followed subsequently by an END IF statement. Second, it is not
permissible to transfer control into a block-IF structure from
outside it.

Practical use of block-IF is illustrated in Example 5-4.

EXAMPLE 5-4

For a simple beam of length L meters supported at each end and
carrying a uniform load of W N/m and a concentrated load of P
Newtons at a distance D from the left end (see Fig. 5-4a), it can be

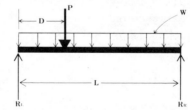

Figure 5-4a. Simple Beam

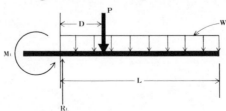

Figure 5-4b. Cantilever Beam

shown that the left and right reactions (i.e., supporting forces) may be computed from the following formulas:

$$R_R = \frac{(P)(D) + \frac{(W)(L)^2}{2}}{L}$$

$$R_L = P + (W)(L) - R_R$$

If, however, the same beam is supported by only a fixed end at the left and no reaction at the right end (see Fig. 5-4b; this is referred to as a cantilever beam), it can be shown that the left vertical reaction and resisting moment may be computed from the following formulas:

$$R_L = P + (W)(L)$$

$$M_L = (P)(D) + \frac{(W)(L)^2}{2}$$

Write a computer program that will read values of P, W, L, D, and a KØDE number from data cards and compute and write out the reactions. A KØDE number of 1 will denote a beam supported at each end, and a KØDE number of 2 will denote a beam supported only by a fixed end. Each data card will contain one value each for P, W, L, D, and KØDE, and there may be any number of data cards with a blank card placed at the end of the data deck.

SOLUTION:
Figure 5-5 gives a flowchart for this problem. The program would be

```
C
CØMMENT--READ INPUT DATA
C
      400 READ(5,500)P,W,XL,D,KØDE
      500 FØRMAT(4F10.0,I2)
C
CØMMENT--CHECK TØ SEE IF LAST CARD HAS
C         BEEN READ--IF SØ, STØP

          IF(XL.LT..001)STØP
C
CØMMENT--DETERMINE WHAT KIND ØF BEAM IT IS
C
          IF(KØDE.EQ.1)THEN
```

```
C
CØMMENT--CØMPUTE AND WRITE REACTIØNS FØR
C          BEAM SUPPØRTED AT EACH END
C
        RR=(P*D+W*XL**2/2.0)/XL
        RL=P+W*XL-RR
        WRITE(6,600)
        WRITE(6,601)P,W,XL,D
        WRITE(6,602)RL,RR
    600 FØRMAT(' SIMPLE BEAM'/)
    601 FØRMAT('  P = ',F10.0,' N'/'  W = ',
        *F10.0,' N/M'/'  L = ',F10.0,
```

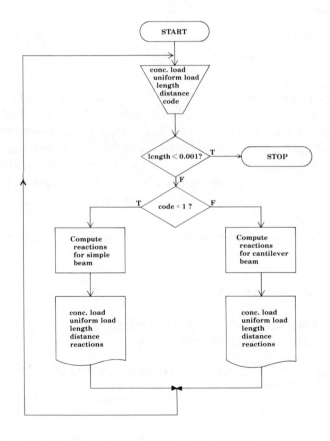

Figure 5-5   Flow Chart for Example 5-4

```
      *' M'/'  D = ',F10.0,' M'/)
  602 FØRMAT('  LEFT REACTIØN = ',F11.1,
      *' N AND RIGHT REACTIØN = ',
      *F11.1,' N'///)
      ELSE
C
CØMMENT--CØMPUTE AND WRITE REACTIØNS FØR
C         BEAM SUPPØRTED ØNLY AT FIXED END
C
      RL=P+W*XL
      RM=P*D+W*XL**2/2.0
      WRITE(6,603)
      WRITE(6,601)P,W,XL,D
      WRITE(6,604)RL,RM
  603 FØRMAT('  CANTILEVER BEAM'/)
  604 FØRMAT('  LEFT REACTIØN = ',F11.1,
      *' N AND LEFT MØMENT =',F11.1,
      *' N-M'///)
      END IF
C
CØMMENT--RETURN TØ READ NEXT CARD
C
      GØ TØ 400
      END
```

Note that the mechanism for terminating the above program is to check after each data card is read to see if the value of XL (length of the beam) is zero, or nearly zero. If it is not, the program continues; if it is, this would indicate that the last card (that is, the blank card) has been read and the program terminates. The value of XL was selected to test for zero because it would never have a value of zero on any data card. One (or more) of the other input data (P, W, D) could conceivably be zero on any data card; hence, none of these should be chosen for the "zero test." Note also that the test does not really check to see if XL is equal to zero but instead checks to see if XL is less than 0.001. The reason for this is that sometimes the computer stores numbers in an unexpected manner. For example, the number 2. may be stored as 1.999999999. When this is compared for equality with a 2. that is stored as 2.000000000, the result is "not equal"; although for all practical purposes, they are equal. Hence, care must be taken when comparing real variables and/or constants for equality. (This is not a problem when integers are compared.)

5-5 PROBLEMS

In each of Problems 5-1 through 5-3, tell what the computer would write.

```
5-1        A=1.00
           B=2.0
           C=3.0
         7 D=A+B+C/3.0
           E=C+5.0
           B=B+1.0
           IF(B.GT.3.0)GØ TØ 6
           GØ TØ 7
         6 WRITE(6,8)A,B,C,D,E
         8 FØRMAT(1X,5F6.0)
```

```
5-2        J=5
           K=10
           L=13
           M=J+K+L/2
        52 L=L+2
           IF(L.EQ.15)J=J+7
           IF(L.NE.15)GØ TØ 55
           GØ TØ 52
        55 WRITE(6,56)K,L,M
        56 FØRMAT(1X,3I5)
```

```
5-3        R=100.
           S=200.
           T=400.
      3000 T=T+1.0
           U=R-S-T**.5
           V=S+T/2.0
           IF(S-R+1.0)1000,1000,2000
      2000 IF(T.GT.5.0)S=0.0
           GØ TØ 3000
      1000 WRITE(6,4000)R,S,T,U,V
      4000 FØRMAT(1X,5F10.0)
```

In each of Problems 5-4 through 5-7, tell what, if anything, is wrong with the statement given.

5-4   IF(X–Y+A)GØ TØ 25

5-5   IF(A.LT.X.LT.500.)W=W+1.0

5-6   IF(NN–50)55,56

5-7   IF(X.LT.5.0.AND.Y.NE.6.2)WRITE(6,6)X,Y,AB

5-8   Revise Problem 4-1 to solve for values of q corresponding to all values of H from 2.0 ft to 5.0 ft in increments of 0.1 ft. Use α equal to 45°. Write the results in tabular form.

5-9   Revise Problem 4-1 to solve for values of q corresponding to all values of α from 40° to 50° in increments of 1°. Use H equal to 2.5 ft.

5-10   Revise Problem 4-5 to read n values of R (that is, R_1, R_2, R_3, ..., R_n) and compute the value of a replacement resistor. An initial data card will give the value of n. Use your own data or those indicated by your instructor.

5-11   Revise Problem 4-6 to solve for values of shaft diameter corresponding to all values of rotation from 3000 rpm to 4000 rpm in increments of 50 rpm. Use 450 hp and an allowable stress of 14,000 lb/in^2.

5-12   Revise Problem 4-6 to read cards each of which contains values of horsepower, rotation, and allowable stress and compute and write out the required shaft diameter. Provide a means of stopping the program when the last data card has been processed. Use the following data:

horsepower	rotation, rpm	allowable stress, lb/in^2
450	3200	15,000
480	3200	14,000
505	4000	16,000
550	3500	14,000
490	3100	14,500

5-13   Revise Problem 4-7 to solve for values of displacement corresponding to all values of time from zero to 50 sec in increments of 5.0 sec. Use an initial velocity of 3.0 cm/sec and an acceleration of 2.5 cm/sec^2.

5-14   Revise Problem 4-7 to read cards each of which contains values of initial velocity, acceleration, and time and compute and write out the displacement. Provide a means of stopping the program when the last data card has been read. Use the following data:

initial velocity, cm/sec	acceleration, cm/sec²	time, sec
3.0	2.9	10.0
3.4	2.9	17.7
6.6	5.0	5.1
7.8	7.8	22.5
10.0	1.0	8.8
5.3	4.4	7.5

5-15 Revise Problem 4-8 to read cards each of which contains values of E, I, and ϕ and compute and write out the power. Use your own data or those indicated by your instructor.

5-16 Revise Problem 4-10 to read cards each of which contains values of the lengths of the three sides of a triangle and compute and write out the area of the triangle. Use your own data or those indicated by your instructor.

6
DØ Loops and Subscripted Variables

6-1 INTRODUCTION

Using the programming techniques presented in the previous five chapters of this book, one can write many computer programs to solve many problems. There is, however, one serious shortcoming and that is the inability to handle easily large amounts of data, including storing of the data in the computer. Heretofore, the only means of storing data is to assign a variable name to each input item; and if large amounts of data are to be stored, a large number of variable names will be required. Certainly, the use of a large number of variable names could become unwieldy.

In order to be able to handle data more easily and more efficiently, Fortran includes the "subscripted variable," which will be covered in detail in this chapter. Subscripted variables are also needed and used in many mathematical operations. Also presented in this chapter is the DØ loop, since it is often used in conjunction with subscripted variables. Special emphasis is given to input and output of subscripted variables, using the "implied DØ loop."

6-2 DØ LOOPS

In the program written for Example 5-3, a sequence of statements like the following occurred:

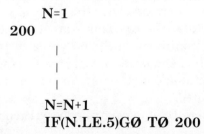

```
      N=1
200
      |
      |
      |
      N=N+1
      IF(N.LE.5)GØ TØ 200
```

This sequence of statements, or a similar one, occurs frequently in programming for the general purpose of causing a program to go through a loop a certain number of times. It occurs so frequently, in fact, that a special technique has been set up to handle the procedure. This technique is called the DØ loop.

Two statements are required to have a DØ loop — one at the beginning of the loop and one at the end. The general form is as follows:

DØ n i=j,k,m

    |

    |

    |

   n

The first statement is characterized by the word DØ, followed by a statement number n. This is followed (without punctuation) by a designation i=j,k,m. The n in the DØ statement must be the statement number of the last statement in the loop. The i (called the "index") in the DØ statement must be an integer variable. This integer variable takes on a different value each time through the loop. The j, k, and m in the DØ statement should be either integer constants or integer variables greater than zero.

The DØ loop functions as follows: When the DØ statement is executed, the value of the index (i) is set initially equal to j. (If j is a variable, it must previously have been defined.) Succeeding statements are then executed until the statement n is reached. After statement n is reached and executed, the value of the index is incremented by m and then compared with the value k. If the value of the index is less than or equal to k, the statements from the DØ statement through statement n are executed again. When statement n is reached and executed again, the value of the index is again incremented by m and then compared with the value of k. If the index is less than or equal to k, the previous statements are executed again. This procedure continues until the value of the index exceeds the value of k. When the latter occurs, the DØ loop has been completed, and the statement after statement n and succeeding statements are executed.

Using a DØ loop, the program of Example 5-3 may be written as follows:

```
CØMMENT--WRITE ØUT CØLUMN HEADINGS
C
          WRITE(6,88)
```

```
        88 FØRMAT('1    RØUGHNESS CØEFF.   SLØPE'
         *'   DEPTH    WIDTH   VELOCITY'/
         *32X,'(FT)    (FT)    (FT/SEC)')
C
CØMMENT--BEGIN DØ LØØP TØ READ 5 CARDS
C
           DØ 300 N=1,5
C
CØMMENT--READ INPUT DATA
C
           READ(5,20)XN,SLØPE,DEPTH,WIDTH
        20 FØRMAT(F5.3,F5.4,2F5.0)
C
CØMMENT--CØMPUTE HYDRAULIC RADIUS
C
           HYRAD=WIDTH*DEPTH/(WIDTH+2.*DEPTH)
C
CØMMENT--CØMPUTE VELØCITY
C
           V=1.486/XN*HYRAD**(2./3.)*SQRT(SLØPE)
C
CØMMENT--WRITE ØUT RESULTS
C
           WRITE(6,8)XN,SLØPE,DEPTH,WIDTH,V
         8 FØRMAT(8X,F9.3,9X,F6.4,F7.0,F9.0,F9.1)
C
CØMMENT--END DØ LØØP
C
       300 CØNTINUE
           STØP
           END
```

A few comments about the DØ loop are needed. The statement numbered n identifies the last statement in the DØ loop. It may be any executable Fortran statement except for control statements (GØ TØ and IF), terminating statements, or a DØ statement. It is convenient, however, to use a CØNTINUE statement as the last statement in a DØ loop. CØNTINUE is simply a dummy command that means "don't perform any computations, just proceed with the next scheduled statement."

The majority of the time, the value of m in a DØ loop is 1. That is, the index is to be incremented by 1 each time through the DØ loop. If the desired value of m is 1, it (and the preceding comma) may be omitted from the DØ statement, and a value of 1 will automatically be used.

In the last program the DØ loop was used only for the purpose of controlling the number of times the statements within the loop were executed. That is, the variable N was used only as a counter and never appeared in any statement. It is possible (and frequently occurs) for the index to appear in statements in the DØ loop. Thus the statements below could have appeared in the DØ loop of the last program

    J=2*N
    WRITE(6,690)J,N
690 FØRMAT(1X,2I4)

Each time through the loop, a new value of J would be computed, and the current value of J and N (the index) would be written out.

It is possible to send program execution out of a DØ loop before the index is satisfied. This could be done as follows:

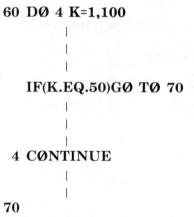

60 DØ 4 K=1,100

    IF(K.EQ.50)GØ TØ 70

4 CØNTINUE

70

In this skeleton of a DØ loop, it is obvious that program execution would "kick out" of the DØ loop when K gets equal to 50, which is before the DØ loop is "satisfied" (i.e., before K gets to be greater than 100).

It is of interest to note that a DØ loop will normally be executed at least once. This is true even if the value of j (in the DØ loop designation i=j,k,m) is larger than the value of k.

Finally, it is possible for one DØ loop to appear within another one. It is illegal though to have one DØ loop begin, another begin, then the first one end, then the second one end. These are illustrated below.

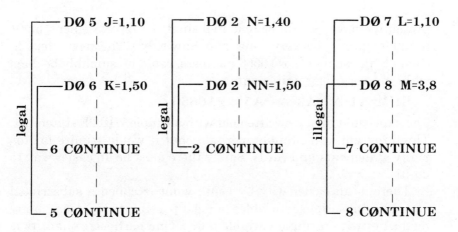

6-3 SINGLE SUBSCRIPTED VARIABLES

Suppose you are given 6666 data cards, each of which contains one number in an F10.2 FØRMAT. It is desired to write a computer program that will read all these 6666 numbers, store them, and compute and write out their sum after storing them.

An extremely long program would result if only the techniques learned thus far were used to write this program. Since it is specified that each number be read and stored, it would be necessary to think up 6666 different variable names. The simplest choice would probably be something like

A1, A2, A3, A4, A5, -----, A6666

These would be 6666 different variable names. Then it would require 6666 READ statements to read and store these variables. This would look like

44 FØRMAT(F10.2)
READ(5,44)A1
READ(5,44)A2
READ(5,44)A3
READ(5,44)A4
READ(5,44)A5
.
.
.
READ(5,44)A6666

(Actually, they could all be read in a single READ statement, but it would certainly be very long and unwieldy.) The next step, to compute the sum of these 6666 numbers, could presumably be done with one very long statement:

SUM=A1+A2+A3+A4+A5+...+A6666

The sum could then be written out with a simple WRITE statement. This program is legitimate, perhaps, but it would require far too many statements and cards. Surely there must be an easier way to do it!

There is an easier way by using what is called a subscripted variable. Subscripted variables make it possible to represent many quantities with a single variable name. One particular quantity is designated by writing a subscript (or subscripts) in parentheses after the variable name. The complete group of quantities is called an *array*, and each individual quantity is called an *element*.

The variable name to designate elements in an array must be chosen in accordance with the previously described rules for naming variables. Elements in any given array must *all* be either integer, real, or alphanumeric, and the variable name of the array must be chosen accordingly (that is, for integer variables, the first letter must be I, J, K, L, M, or N).

In the last problem, an array, designated by the variable name A, containing 6666 elements, could be established. The elements in this array would be A(1), A(2), A(3), A(4), A(5), ..., A(6666). The difference between this notation and the previous one (A1, A2, A3, etc.) is that in this notation, the variable name itself is A, but it can represent many quantities using a subscript; whereas in the previous notation, *each* entry (A1, A2, A3, A4, etc.) is a separate variable name.

The subscript part of a subscripted variable should be an integer value greater than zero. It may be either a constant, a variable, or another expression. For example, the 20th element in array ABJ could be designated either ABJ(20) or ABJ(5*4), or ABJ(IX) provided IX is equal to 20.

The subscripted variable can be used in Fortran statements just like any other variable. It can appear alone on the left side of an arithmetic assignment statement, or it can appear in an expression on the right side.

Whenever a subscripted variable is used in a main program, it is necessary to state initially the size of the array (i.e., the maximum number of elements in the array). This can be done with a DIMENSIØN statement. The DIMENSIØN statement simply has the word DIMENSIØN followed by a list of variables to be subscripted, each of which must indicate by an integer constant in parentheses the maximum number of elements in the array. For example, suppose three variables, AA, JØHN, and ØØØ22, are to be subscripted. AA will have a maximum of 30 elements; JØHN will have a maximum of 200; and ØØØ22 will have a maximum of 16. The necessary DIMENSIØN statement would be

DIMENSIØN AA(30),JØHN(200),ØØØ22(16)

The DIMENSIØN statement, like other Fortran statements, must begin in or after column 7. The DIMENSIØN statement should come at the beginning of the program. Also, each subscripted variable could be dimensioned in a separate DIMENSIØN statement.

With a knowledge of the subscripted variable, the previous program may be written:

```
    DIMENSIØN A(6666)
 44 FØRMAT(F10.2)
    SUM=0.
    DØ 88 LLL=1,6666
    READ(5,44)A(LLL)
 88 CØNTINUE
    DØ 64 KM2=1,6666
    SUM=SUM+A(KM2)
 64 CØNTINUE
    WRITE(6,45)SUM
 45 FØRMAT(' SUM =',F12.2)
    STØP
    END
```

This program begins with a DIMENSIØN statement, which indicates that the variable A will be subscripted with a maximum of 6666 elements. The value of a variable named SUM is set initially equal to zero. (This step is included because on many machines the storages for variables are not erased after use, and it is necessary to zero variables that are to be used for summing, integration, etc. In other words, the storage location for the variable SUM might have a non-zero value left over from a previous program; and if it is not zeroed initially, the leftover value would be included in the computation of the sum in the second DØ loop. This step is similar to clearing a manual calculator prior to using it to add a series of numbers.) Then a DØ loop is utilized to read in the required data. According to the DØ statement, the value of the index, LLL, is set initially equal to 1. The next statement indicates to read a card according to FØRMAT 44 and give the value to the variable A(1), since LLL equals 1. The next statement is 88, the last statement in the DØ loop, so the value of LLL is incremented by 1, giving 2. This value is compared to 6666. Since it is not greater than 6666, the statements in the DØ loop will be executed again. The READ statement will cause the next data card to be read, and the value will be given to the variable A(2), since LLL equals 2 now. This procedure will be repeated until the DØ loop is satisfied and all values have been read and stored in the array. The reader should understand that the first DØ loop accomplishes this.

When the first DØ loop is completed, a second one is encountered immediately. The second DØ loop computes the sum of all the numbers. When this DØ loop is encountered, the value of the index KM2 is set initially equal to 1. [The index (KM2) could have been the same as the index of the previous DØ loop (LLL).] The next statement computes the sum of the "old value of SUM" plus A(1), since KM2 is equal to 1. The "old value of SUM," which is zero initially, is added to the value of A(1), giving a new value of SUM. The next statement completes the DØ loop, so the value of KM2 is incremented by 1, giving 2. This value is compared to 6666. Since it is not greater than 6666, the statements in the DØ loop will be executed again. The next statement adds the "old value of SUM" and the value A(2), since KM2 equals 2 now. This procedure will be repeated until the DØ loop is satisfied and the total sum has been computed. The next steps are to write out the result and terminate the program. The reader should understand how this program accomplishes the desired result.

This program could have been written with only one DØ loop. The sum could have been computed as each number was read. However, the statement of the problem specified that all data must be read and stored prior to computing the sum of the numbers. For this reason, two DØ loops were used.

Once these values have been read and stored, as above, it is possible to do a number of things with them such as computing the sum, mean, standard deviation, sorting the numbers in ascending or descending order, and so on. Example 6-1 illustrates further the value of the subscripted variable in Fortran.

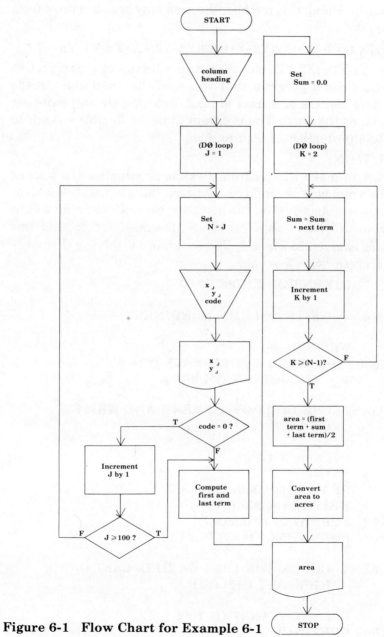

Figure 6-1 Flow Chart for Example 6-1

EXAMPLE 6-1

In surveying, the area of a tract of land can be calculated by the coordinate method if the coordinates of each corner of the tract are known. Using this method, the area may be determined from the equation

$A = 1/2[X1(Y2-Yn)+X2(Y3-Y1)+X3(Y4-Y2)+....+Xn(Y1-Yn_{-1})]$

where (X1,Y1), (X2,Y2), etc. are the coordinates of the respective corners. Write a program that will read the coordinates of the respective corners of a tract of land and compute and write out the area of the tract. The program must be flexible enough to handle any number of coordinates.

SOLUTION:

In order to make the program flexible as stipulated, a scheme will be employed whereby a non-zero integer number will be punched in column 80 on the last data card. (Column 80 will be blank on all other data cards.) A flowchart for solving this problem is given in Fig. 6-1. The program for solving this problem is given below.

```
        DIMENSIØN X(100),Y(100)
C
CØMMENT--WRITE CØLUMN HEADINGS .
C
        WRITE(6,999)
    999 FØRMAT('1X-CØØRDINATE (FT)'
      *'     Y-CØØRDINATE (FT)')
C
CØMMENT--USE DØ LØØP TØ READ AND WRITE
C         INPUT DATA
C
        DØ 1000 J=1,100
        N=J
        READ(5,1001)X(J),Y(J),LAST
        WRITE(6,1002)X(J),Y(J)
   1001 FØRMAT(2F10.0,59X,I1)
   1002 FØRMAT(5X,F10.1,13X,F10.1)
C
CØMMENT--CHECK FØR LAST CARD IF LAST CARD,
C         KICK ØUT ØF LØØP
C
        IF(LAST.NE.0)GØ TØ 1003
   1000 CØNTINUE
```

```
C
CØMMENT--CØMPUTE FIRST AND LAST TERMS WITHIN
C          BRACKETS
C
  1003 TERM1=X(1)*(Y(2)-Y(N))
       TERMN=X(N)*(Y(1)-Y(N-1))
C
CØMMENT--USE DØ LØØP TØ CØMPUTE SUM ØF ØTHER
C          TERMS WITHIN BRACKETS
C
       SUM=0.
       DØ 1004 K=2,N-1
       SUM=SUM+X(K)*(Y(K+1)-Y(K-1))
  1004 CØNTINUE
C
CØMMENT--CØMPUTE AREA IN SQ FT AND IN ACRES
C
       AREA=(TERM1+SUM+TERMN)/2.
       ACRES=AREA/43560.
C
CØMMENT--WRITE ANSWERS
C
       WRITE(6,1005)AREA,ACRES
  1005 FØRMAT(//' AREA =',F10.0,' SQ FT OR ',
      *F6.0,' ACRES.')
       STØP
       END
```

The preceding program would be considerably more difficult if subscripted variables were not available. Some comments regarding specific parts of this program follow.

First of all, since it is not known, when the program is written, how many data cards will actually be read when the program is executed, the program is set up to read up to 100 cards. As each card is read, a check is made (by looking for a non-zero integer in column 80 on the card) to see if the card is the last one. As the DØ loop is carried out, successive values of X- and Y- coordinates are read until the last card is encountered, whereupon execution moves out of the DØ loop to statement number 1003. As written this program would not work if there are more than 100 X- and Y- coordinates, but it could easily be altered (by increasing in the DIMENSIØN statement the sizes of the arrays and increasing the limit of the DØ loop) to work for more than 100 coordinates.

Since it is necessary to know later in the program how many X- and Y- coordinates were read, the statement N=J was inserted between the DØ and READ statements. As a result, when the last data card is read and execution moves out of the DØ loop to statement 1003, the value of N will be equal to the number of X- and Y- coordinates.

The actual computation of the area begins with statement number 1003. Since the first term in the equation for area contains Yn and the last term contains Y1, these two terms are computed separately. The sum of the remaining terms in the equation for area is computed by the second DØ loop. Note that the index of this DØ loop varies from 2 to (N-1).

6-4 DOUBLE SUBSCRIPTED VARIABLES

The single subscripted variable was introduced in the previous section. In some instances, it is advantageous to use two (or more) subscripts to refer to an array. A double subscripted variable can be thought of as representing the elements of a two-dimensional array composed of horizontal rows and vertical columns. The first subscript refers to the row number, and the second to the column number. As an example, an array of four columns and two rows might be expressed in mathematical notation as

$$g_{1,1} \quad g_{1,2} \quad g_{1,3} \quad g_{1,4}$$

$$g_{2,1} \quad g_{2,2} \quad g_{2,3} \quad g_{2,4}$$

Corresponding Fortran notation would be G(1,1), G(2,1), G(1,2), G(2,2), G(1,3), G(2,3), G(1,4), and G(2,4). One must keep in mind that the Fortran designations above are really Fortran variables — i.e., quantities that are given a name and (sometimes) allowed to vary in a program.

Double subscripted variables are useful in a number of ways. Ordinary matrix operations can be handled easily using double subscripted variables. Another use is afforded when it is necessary to refer to each element in a large data set by identifying each of two parameters.

As an example of the use of a double subscripted variable, consider the following. In highway construction, it is often necessary to obtain quantities of earth for roadfill. To avoid the large expense of hauling earth long distances by truck, earth is often purchased from nearby landowners, with pricing done on a

per unit volume basis. This means, of course, that someone, usually
an engineer or a surveyor, must determine the volume of earth
removed from the area (which is called a "borrow pit"). An approximate method for computing the volume of earth removed from a
borrow pit involves laying out a grid system, such as that shown in
Fig. 6-2, and determining ground elevations at the various grid

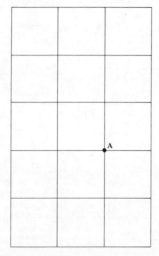

**Figure 6-2   Grid System for Determining Volume
of Earth Removed from Borrow Pit**

points. A double subscripted variable can be conveniently used here
to handle the elevation data. For example, a double subscripted
variable ELEV could be established and dimensioned as ELEV(6,4).
The first subscript identifies the row and the second, the column
which a particular elevation represents. Thus in Fig. 6-2, the point
indicated by A is in the 4th row and the third column of the grid;
hence, it would be represented by ELEV(4,3).

The reader should understand that the designation ELEV(4,3) is
simply the label for a particular location in the computer's memory.
It is actually one of 24 (in this particular example) locations
associated with the variable ELEV. The actual ground elevation at
this point is the datum that would be stored in this location (and
presumably used later in computation).

Example 6-2 demonstrates the advantageous use of the double
subscripted variable.

EXAMPLE 6-2
As indicated previously, the volume of earth removed from a

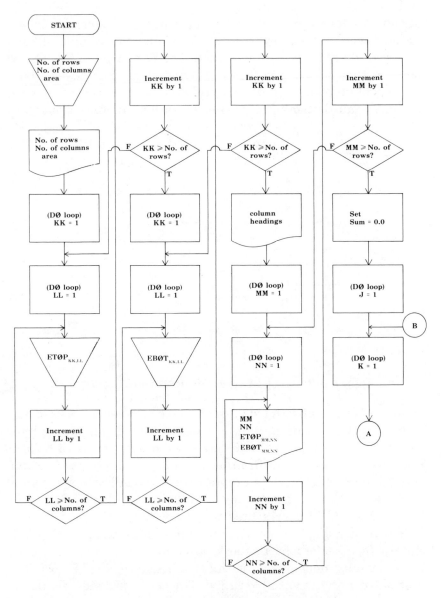

Figure 6-3   Flow Chart for Example 6-2

borrow pit can be obtained using a grid system as shown in Fig. 6-2. The method is to determine the ground elevation of each grid point initially and then to determine the ground elevation of each grid point after the earth has been removed. The difference between these two elevations at a particular point is the "cut" at

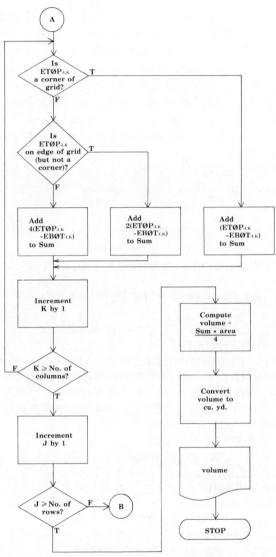

Figure 6-3 (Continued)

that point. The volume of earth removed from a square (or rectangular) area of the grid can be approximated by multiplying the average of the cuts at the four corners of the square (or rectangle) by the surface area of the square (or rectangle). Rather than compute the volume of each individual square (or rectangular) area in this manner, a short cut method can be used to compute the total volume whereby the cut at each corner is multiplied by the number of squares containing that particular corner, these products added, and the resulting sum divided by 4 and multiplied by the area of each square (or rectangular) area.

With this background, write a computer program that will read initially an integer telling how many rows there are in the grid, another integer telling how many columns there are in the grid, and the area of each square (or rectangle). The program should then read the initial ground elevations of the grid points followed by the ground elevations after all earth has been removed. The program should then compute the volume of earth removed by the procedure related above.

SOLUTION:

A flowchart for solving this problem is given in Fig. 6-3. The program for solving this problem is given below.

```
      DIMENSIØN ETØP(100,100),EBØT(100,100)
C
CØMMENT--READ AND WRITE INPUT DATA
C
      READ(5,2000)NRØW,NCØL,AREA
 2000 FØRMAT(2I5,F10.0)
      WRITE(6,2001)NRØW,NCØL,AREA
 2001 FØRMAT('1EARTHWØRK CØMPUTATION'//
     *I4,' ROWS AND',I4,' CØLUMNS'//' AREA OF',
     *' EACH GRID AREA IS ',F10.0,' SQ FT'//)
      DØ 2002 KK=1,NRØW
      DØ 2003 LL=1,NCØL
      READ(5,2004)ETØP(KK,LL)
 2004 FØRMAT(F10.1)
 2003 CØNTINUE
 2002 CØNTINUE
      DØ 2005 KK=1,NRØW
      DØ 2006 LL=1,NCØL
      READ(5,2004)EBØT(KK,LL)
 2006 CØNTINUE
 2005 CØNTINUE
      WRITE(6,2007)
 2007 FØRMAT(' RØW   CØLUMN   TØP ELEV.',
     *' BØTTØM ELEV.')
      DØ 2008 MM=1,NRØW
      DØ 2009 NN=1,NCØL
      WRITE(6,2010)MM,NN,ETØP(MM,NN),EBØT(MM,NN)
 2010 FØRMAT(1X,I3,6X,I4,F13.1,F15.1)
```

```
      2009 CØNTINUE
      2008 CØNTINUE
C
CØMMENT--CØMPUTE SUM ØF CUTS
C
           SUM=0.
           DØ 2011 J=1,NRØW
           DØ 2012 K=1,NCØL
C
CØMMENT--IF PØINT IS CØRNER ØF GRID, ADD CUT
C            TØ SUM AND GØ TØ END ØF LØØP
C
           IF((J.EQ.1.AND.K.EQ.1).OR.(J.EQ.1.AND.K.EQ.
          *NCØL).OR.(J.EQ.NRØW.AND.K.EQ.1).OR.(J.EQ.NRØW
          *.AND.K.EQ.NCØL))SUM=SUM+(ETØP(J,K)-EBØT(J,K))
           IF((J.EQ.1.AND.K.EQ.1).OR.(J.EQ.1.AND.K.EQ.
          *NCØL).OR.(J.EQ.NRØW.AND.K.EQ.1).OR.(J.EQ.NRØW
          *.AND.K.EQ.NCØL))GØ TØ 2012
C
CØMMENT--IF PØINT IS ØN EDGE ØF GRID
C            (BUT NØT A CØRNER), ADD TWICE THE CUT
C            TØ SUM AND GØ TØ END ØF LØØP
C
           IF(J.EQ.1.ØR.J.EQ.NRØW.ØR.K.EQ.1.ØR.K.EQ.NCØL)
          *SUM=SUM+2.*(ETØP(J,K)-EBØT(J,K))
           IF(J.EQ.1.ØR.J.EQ.NRØW.ØR.K.EQ.1.ØR.K.EQ.NCØL)
          *GØ TØ 2012
C
CØMMENT--FØR ØTHER PØINTS, ADD FØUR TIMES THE
C            CUT TØ SUM
C
           SUM=SUM+4.*(ETØP(J,K)-EBØT(J,K))
      2012 CØNTINUE
      2011 CØNTINUE
C
CØMMENT--CØMPUTE VØLUME FRØM SUM AND
C            WRITE RESULT
C
           VØL=SUM/4.*AREA
           VCUYD=VØL/27.
           WRITE(6,2013)VØL,VCUYD
      2013 FØRMAT(///' VØLUME IS ',F10.0,' CU FT ØR ',
          *F9.0,' CU YD')
           STØP
           END
```

In reviewing the program written for Example 6-2, one can make several observations. The DIMENSIØN statement establishes two 2-dimensional arrays (i.e., double subscripted variables) — one to store initial elevations at grid points and the other to store final (after excavation) elevations at grid points. Since it is not known when the program is written how many grid points will be in a specific application of the program, it is not known precisely how to dimension these variables. (Subscripts in a DIMENSIØN statement in a main program cannot be variables; they must be constants.) In this program, the arrays were dimensioned as 100 by 100, on the assumption that no grid larger than this would be encountered. In many applications, only a part of the 100 by 100 array would be used.

The first READ statement in the program reads the numbers of rows and columns in the particular grid as well as the area of each square (or rectangular) area. Thus at execution time, the numbers of rows and columns are known immediately and are used as limits on DØ loops in subsequent computations.

The first two (nested) DØ loops read and store the initial elevations at grid points, and the next two read and store the final (after excavation) elevations at grid points. The next two DØ loops write out the input elevation data. The exact manner in which these data are read will be discussed more thoroughly in the next section.

The remainder of the program actually computes the volume of earth removed. The last two DØ loops compute the sum of all cuts at grid points with those on the four corners of the overall grid multiplied by 1 (since those grid points are common to only one square or rectangular area), those on the perimeter of the overall grid that are not one of the four corners of the overall grid multiplied by 2 (since those grid points are common to two square or rectangular areas), and all remaining grid points multiplied by 4 (since those grid points are common to four square or rectangular areas). Note well how this is accomplished. If a given grid point is one of the four corners of the overall grid, it is "intercepted" by the first IF statement in the loop and its cut is added to the sum. The second IF statement then sends control to the end of the loop. If a given grid point is on the perimeter of the overall grid but is not one of the four corners, it is "intercepted" by the third IF statement in the loop and its cut multiplied by 2 is added to the sum. The fourth

IF statement then sends control to the end of the loop. Other grid points will have their cuts multiplied by 4 and added to the sum. This is accomplished by the statement preceding statement number 2012. Note that this statement is executed only if all of the four preceding IF statements are "not true." (These DØ loops could probably be coded a bit more efficiently by using the Block-IF feature, but it was not done here because this feature is not universally available.)

When these DØ loops are satisfied, the volume is determined by dividing the sum just computed by 4 and multiplying by the area of each square (or rectangular) area. This gives the volume in cubic feet, assuming input values are in feet. Since volume of earthwork is often expressed in cubic yards, the volume in cubic feet was divided by 27 to determine the number of cubic yards. The final step is, of course, to write out the answers.

6-5 IMPLIED DØ LOOPS

Consider again the first six DØ loops in the program written for Example 6-2. These are all used to read or write the data in the 2-dimensional arrays. The first two DØ loops cause input data to be read for array ETØP. The first time the READ statement within these loops is executed, the value of KK is 1 and the value of LL is also 1. Hence, the value read from the data card is stored in ETØP(1,1). Note that only one value will be read from the data card and that from columns 1 through 10. This would be true even if the FØRMAT were 5F10.0 or 8F10.0, since the READ statement, when executed calls for only one value to be read. The second time this READ statement is executed, the value of KK is still 1; but the value of LL will be 2. Hence, the value read from the next data card will be stored in ETØP(1,2). Again, only one value will be read and that from columns 1 through 10 of the second data card. This continues until the inner DØ loop is satisfied (i.e., until LL exceeds NCØL). Control then passes out of the inner loop, to statement number 2002, which indicates the end of the outer DØ loop. At this point KK will be incremented to 2 and, unless that satisfies the outer loop, the outer loop will be executed again. The first statement encountered, however, is the beginning of the inner DØ loop, which sets LL equal to 1 again. Thus, with LL equal to 1 and KK equal to 2, the READ statement will be executed again and the value read from the next

data card will be stored in ETØP(2,1). The next time this READ
statement is executed, the value of KK will still be 2 and the value of
LL will also be 2. Hence, the value read from the next card will be
stored in ETØP(2,2). This continues until both loops have been
satisfied.

It should be apparent now that reading all data into the ETØP
array in the manner described above will require a number of cards
equal to NRØW times NCØL, since only one value is read from each
card. The same is true for the reading of the EBØT array. This
certainly seems wasteful in terms of the number of data cards
required. Considerable savings in cards would accrue if more than
one input value could be put on each data card. This can be done
easily using an "implied DØ."

An implied DØ is similar to a regular DØ loop in that an "index"
is allowed to vary in the general form i=j,k,m, but this varying must
occur only within a READ or a WRITE statement. For example,
assume the first two DØ loops in the program written for Example
6-2 are replaced by the following:

    DØ 2002 KK=1,NRØW
    READ(5,2004)(ETØP(KK,LL),LL=1,NCØL)
2004 FØRMAT(6F10.0)
2002 CØNTINUE

The READ statement here contains the implied DØ loop. Note the
form required, with both the subscripted variable and the DØ
indicator enclosed in parentheses.

When the DØ statement above is executed, index KK is set equal
to 1. When the READ statement is executed, KK has the value 1; but
the value of LL must vary from 1 to NCØL. Suppose the value of
NCØL is 6. In this case, what the READ statement really requires
is that six values be read: ETØP(1,1),ETØP(1,2),ETØP(1,3),
ETØP(1,4),ETØP(1,5),ETØP(1,6). With the indicated FØRMAT of
6F10.0, all six values will be read from a single data card. (Note
carefully that the READ statement above requires that six values
be read — assuming NCØL equal to 6 — every time the READ
statement is executed; whereas the READ statement within the
first two DØ loops in the program written for Example 6-2 requires
that only one value be read every time the READ statement is
executed.) After the READ statement is executed, the end of the DØ
loop is encountered, and the value of KK will be incremented to 2. If
the DØ loop has not been satisfied, it will be repeated and the
READ statement will be executed again. This time, the value of KK

will be 2, and the next six values will be read: ETØP(2,1),ETØP(2,2), ETØP(2,3),ETØP(2,4),ETØP(2,5),ETØP(2,6). Thus, this routine reads the data one row at a time.

Suppose the FØRMAT in the previous DØ loop is changed to 8F10.0, with everything else remaining the same (including the assumption that NCØL is 6). Would this affect the manner in which the data are read? The answer is no. When the READ statement is executed, it still causes, in effect, the six values [ETØP(1,1), ETØP(1,2),ETØP(1,3),ETØP(1,4),ETØP(1,5),ETØP(1,6)] to be read. Although a FØRMAT of 8F10.0 provides for eight values on the card, the READ statement causes only six values to be read and therefore only six values will be read upon each execution of the DØ loop. The six values would, of course, be read from columns 1 through 60 on the data card.

Suppose, however, the FØRMAT in the previous DØ loop is changed to 4F10.0, with everything else remaining the same (including the assumption that NCØL is 6). Would this affect the manner in which the data are read? The answer is yes. When the READ statement is executed, the same six values will be read. This FØRMAT, however, allows for only four values to be read from a card. As explained in Chap. 3, all six values will be read, with the first four coming from columns 1 through 40 on the first card and the last two coming from columns 1 through 20 on the second card. If this DØ loop is executed again for KK equal to 2, four values [ETØP(2,1),ETØP(2,2),ETØP(2,3),ETQP(2,4)] will be read from the third card and two [ETØP(2,5),ETØP(2,6)], from the fourth card.

As mentioned previously, the routine being considered reads the data by rows. Suppose, however, it is desired to read the data by columns. This can be accomplished by modifying the previous DØ loop as follows:

```
      DØ 2002 LL=1,NCØL
      READ(5,2004)(ETØP(KK,LL),KK=1,NRØW)
 2004 FØRMAT(6F10.0)
 2002 CØNTINUE
```

Note that, in this DØ loop, the second subscript remains equal to 1 while the first subscript varies from 1 to NRØW the first time the READ statement is executed. Hence, if NRØW is equal to 5, the values read would be assigned to ETØP(1,1),ETØP(2,1),ETØP(3,1), ETØP(4,1),ETØP(5,1). This represents, of course, the first column. Hence, the data are being read by columns. It will be left to the reader to examine this further (for example, for additional executions of the DØ loop and the READ statement).

One additional consideration is necessary with regard to input/output of subscripted variables. Normally, if a variable is subscripted in a program (as indicated by the DIMENSIØN statement), it must always appear with a subscript or subscripts in that program. The notable exception is in the case of input/output statements. If a subscripted variable appears in either an input or output statement without a subscript, the entire array will be either read or written. For example, suppose the variable SAT has been dimensioned SAT(20). The following statement would cause the entire array to be read:

READ(5,8)SAT

This statement would cause the same thing to happen as would the following:

READ(5,8)(SAT(J),J=1,20)

Both of these READ statements would cause 20 values to be read, but the arrangement of the numbers on the data cards would depend on the associated FØRMAT statement.

In the case of a double subscripted variable, the question arises as to the order in which the data would be read or written if the variable appears in an input or output statement. The answer is that they would be read by columns. Thus, if SUM is dimensioned SUM(3,3), the following statement would cause the entire array to be written:

WRITE(6,10)SUM

Furthermore, the data would be written in the following order: SUM(1,1),SUM(2,1),SUM(3,1),SUM(1,2),SUM(2,2),SUM(3,2), SUM(1,3),SUM(2,3),SUM(3,3). This statement would be equivalent to the following one:

WRITE(6,10)((SUM(J,JJ),J=1,3),JJ=1,3)

The foregoing material presented in this section should demonstrate that care must be exercised in reading and writing data in the form of subscripted variables. The programmer must assure that data are punched on data cards according to both the READ statement and the FØRMAT statement. For example, if FØRMAT statement number 8 associated with the last READ statement above was (F4.0) but the 20 data were all punched on a single data card, the data would not get read correctly. (In order to be read correctly using this FØRMAT, each datum would have to appear on a separate card, thus requiring 20 data cards. Why?) Beginning programmers make many mistakes of this type. Remember: the computer is not a mind reader. It will read data exactly as you specify — not according to what you intended but incorrectly coded.

6-6 PROBLEMS

In each of Problems 6-1 through 6-5, tell what, if anything, is wrong with the statement given.

6-1   DØ 55, J=1,M,N

6-2   DØ 88 A=B,C,4

6-3   DØ 100 5=I,J,K

6-4   DØ 9 M7=M8,M9

6-5   DØ N K=1.1,1000,3

In each of Problems 6-6 through 6-8, tell what the computer would write.

6-6   DIMENSIØN A(4)
         DØ 5 K=1,4
       5 A(K)=K**3
         WRITE(6,6)A
       6 FØRMAT(1X,4F10.0)

6-7   DIMENSIØN I(2,3)
         DØ 99 K=1,2
         DØ 99 L=1,3
         I(K,L)=3*K+4*L
         M=2/11
      99 CØNTINUE
         WRITE(6,6)I,M
       6 FØRMAT(1X,8I5)

6-8   DIMENSIØN W(3)
         DØ 5 KK=1,3
         N=KK
         W(KK)=KK+3
         IF(KK.EQ.2)W(2)=0.0
       5 CØNTINUE
         DØ 6 L=1,2
       6 W(L)=W(L)**2
         WRITE(6,66)W,N

    66 FØRMAT(3F10.0,I5)

6-9   Rework Problem 5-8 using a DØ loop.

6-10 Rework Problem 5-9 using a DØ loop.

6-11 Rework Problem 5-11 using a DØ loop.

6-12 Rework Problem 5-12 using a DØ loop.

6-13 Rework Problem 5-13 using a DØ loop.

6-14 A manufacturing company maintains a current inventory in which each item has an identification number and a corresponding number that indicates how many of that item are in stock. Write a program that will:

(a) read an unknown (at the time the program is written) number of cards that give the initial inventory;

(b) read an unknown (at the time the program is written) number of cards each of which contains an identification number and a corresponding number that indicates how many of that item were sold (removed from inventory); and

(c) compute and write out the new inventory.

Provide a means of stopping the reading of data at the appropriate times in (a) and (b) above. Have the program write an appropriate message if a nonexistent identification number is read in (b) above.

6-15 Revise the program of Problem 6-14 to include a minimum inventory corresponding with each identification number. When the program is run, if enough of any items are sold to reduce the number on hand below the minimum inventory, have the computer write a message indicating how many are needed to bring the number of those items up to minimum.

6-16 Revise the program of Problem 6-15 to include a 12 character name corresponding with each inventory item.

6-17 Write a program that will read and store the x- and y-coordinates of an unknown (at the time the program is written) number of points on the earth's surface. The program will then read successive pairs of numbers identifying two of these points and, in each case, compute and write out the distance between the two points. Use the following data:

Point Number	x-coordinate, m	y-coordinate, m
23	33,456.7	36,995.0
88	26,555.9	18,004.5
53	11,109.0	22,599.5
190	7,908.2	4,900.0
1	665.3	5,088.1

20	10,045.5	8,864.0
390	5,449.0	18,040.3

Points between which distance is to be found
23 and 53
88 and 190
20 and 1
390 and 53

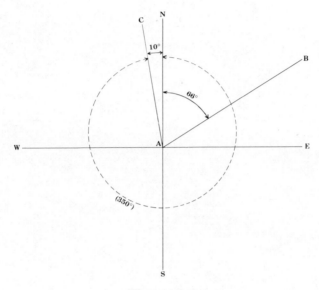

Figure 6-4

6-18 The direction from one point on the earth's surface to another one can be indicated by giving the azimuth of the line. The azimuth of a line is the clockwise angle measured from a north/south line to the line itself. Thus, in Fig. 6-4 the azimuth of line AB is 66° and that of line AC is 350°. Revise the program written for Problem 6-17 to compute the azimuth of the line joining the two points in addition to determining the distance between the two points.

6-19 Write a program that will read the coefficients of an equation of the form

$$a_n x^n + \dots + a_2 x^2 + a_1 x + a_0 = y$$

and a value of x. The program is to compute the value of y. The program must work for any value of n.

6-20 Write a program that is capable of reading and storing the highest temperature, the lowest temperature, and the amount of precipitation for each day from January 1, 1900 to December 31, 1999. The program should then be able to write out the highest temperature, the lowest temperature, and the amount of precipitation for any date that is input to the program.

7

The Statement Function and Subprograms

7-1 INTRODUCTION

As the student programmer develops larger Fortran programs, often he or she will realize that certain procedures are performed repeatedly in the programs. Even though a great advantage of using computers is that they can perform many calculations very quickly, the programmer should always try to write efficient programs, rather than allowing the computer to be used as a "number cruncher" without regard to wastage of computer time or memory. Thus repeated coding of the same steps should be avoided.

One method of economizing in computer time and memory used is to allow certain generic segments of coding to be grouped and used when needed. In addition to saving programming time, this grouping concept also will separate and clarify the functions of the overall programs — like delegation of duties. One group of statements will perform this function; a second group, that function; etc.

In Fortran there are four programming entities that allow this grouping:
1) the built-in function
2) the statement function
3) the external function
4) the subroutine

The *built-in* function, which is essentially of the same composition as an External Function, has been described in Chap. 2 and will not be repeated here. The External Function and the Subroutine will be referred to as "subprograms" that may be referenced either from the master group of statements (the main program) or from other subprograms.

7-2 THE STATEMENT FUNCTION

As the name implies, this concept involves just one Fortran statement. The statement function allows the programmer to define initially a particular computation and then to carry it out at some point in the program execution by simply referring to the function's name. The statement function itself is just a "dummy" statement, which conveys the exact computation that is to be performed later — during the program execution — at one or more points in the program. Usually the computation will be made on different data each time it is repeated. A statement function may only be used within the program in which it is placed.

If a statement function is to be utilized in a program, it must be defined at the beginning of the program — before any executable statements. It is defined by writing a statement of the form a=b, where "a" is the name of the function and "b" is a Fortran expression. The name of the statement function is selected by the programmer and must conform to the rules for naming variables, since the value of expression "b" will be assigned to the name "a" as in an arithmetic assignment statement. The name of the function must be followed by one or more dummy arguments enclosed in parentheses. If more than one argument is necessary, they are separated by commas within the parentheses. None of the dummy arguments may be subscripted variables. The right side of the statement function, "b", must be a Fortran expression consisting of constants and/or variables including the dummy arguments of the left side of the statement function. The right side also may contain references to subscripted variables, built-in and external functions, and other previously defined statement functions. Each variable that is referenced must be either a dummy argument or a variable that is defined in the same program unit — either a main program or a subprogram.

A statement function is referenced by using its name in a Fortran expression in the same program unit. Four steps occur when a statement function is referenced:

1) The actual arguments — those used in the Fortran expression that contains the reference — are evaluated. An actual argument may be either a constant or some other Fortran expression. (Actual arguments in subprogram references may also be constants or other Fortran expressions.)

2) The values of the actual arguments are associated with the

dummy arguments.

3) The expression "b", that is, the right hand side of the original equation, is evaluated.

4) The value of the expression "b" is changed, if necessary, to agree in type with the name of the statement function.

After these steps, the value computed is used in the Fortran expression that referenced the statement function.

Consider the following example. Assume that the value of w is to be computed several times in a program for different values of x, y, and z according to the equation

$$w=5(xy)^5+4(yz)^4+(xyz)^2$$

This might be set up as a statement function with the following definition statement:

W(X,Y,Z)=5.*(X*Y)**5+4.*(Y*Z)**4+(X*Y*Z)**2

The name of this function is W, and the dummy arguments are X, Y, and Z. The variable names X, Y, and Z show how the actual arguments (supplied during execution of the program by a referencing expression) are to be used in the expression on the right above. To demonstrate that the variables X, Y, and Z are dummies, the above statement function definition could have been written instead as:

W(A,B95,DUMMY)=5.*(A*B95)**5+4.*(B95*DUMMY)**4
+(A*B95*DUMMY)**2

The dummy argument names may also be used freely in the remainder of the program as variable names without concern for the fact that they are used in the definition statement.

Using the first statement function definition statement above, suppose it is desired to use the function W in a program for X=1.1, Y=2.1, and Z=3.7. Also assume that later in the same program some value S^2 is to be added to the value of four times the value of function W for X=0.926, Y=X, and Z=XYJ7(10) where X and XYJ7(10) are variables that have been given values elsewhere in the program. This could be accomplished as follows:

```
    W(X,Y,Z)=5.*(X*Y)**5+4.*(Y*Z)**4+(X*Y*Z)**2
20  VALUE=W(1.1,2.1,3.7)
30  AMØUNT=S**2+4.*W(0.926,X,XYJ7(10))
```

The first statement above is the definition statement, which defines the exact computation to be made in terms of X, Y, and Z. Both statements 20 and 30 involve Fortran expressions that reference statement function W. In statement 20 the Fortran expression is simply function W evaluated for X=1.1, Y=2.1, and Z=3.7. These values will be substituted into the expression on the right side of the function definition statement to obtain the desired value of W. The variable VALUE will then be assigned the value of W. Notice that the function W(3.7,2.1,1.1) would not have the same value as W in statement 20 even though the actual arguments are the same. Why?

Statement 30 contains a reference to the value of W in which each X variable in the definition statement equals 0.926; each Y variable has the value of program variable X (not 0.926); and each Z variable has the value of the 10th element of the subscripted variable XYJ7. This time the corresponding value for W will be multiplied by 4., and that product added to the value of the square of variable S. That sum will then be the value assigned to the variable AMØUNT. It is important to note that the actual argument X in the second term of the expression in statement 30 bears no relation to the dummy argument X of the statement function definition. What actually occurs in statement 30 is that the value of variable X in the program is substituted in the statement function in every position that dummy variable Y occurs.

In both references (statements 20 and 30) note that there is agreement between the actual arguments and the dummy arguments in order, number, and type. By "number" is meant that the actual argument list and the dummy argument list must contain the same number of arguments. By "type" is meant that the arguments in the actual argument list agree one by one by type (real or integer) with the arguments in the dummy argument list. To illustrate consider this statement which is added to the previous program:

40 QUANT=W(.875,XYJ7,3)

If this statement was executed, the integer constant 3 would be associated with the real dummy argument Z, and this association would disagree in "type". This erroneous association might cause an error condition and should be avoided. (It could be avoided by placing a decimal after the 3 thereby making it a real argument.)

7-3 THE FUNCTIØN SUBPROGRAM

In the preceding example, the utility of the statement function is obvious. Sometimes, however, the situation arises in which it would be useful to use a statement function, but the function definition would be so involved that it could not be defined by a single statement. Also, the use of a statement function is limited to use only in the program unit in which it is defined. In such cases subprograms may be used. Subprograms are grouped sets of Fortran statements usually designed to perform computations that are repeated in an overall Fortran program. Subprograms are separate program-like entities, having their own variables, storage locations, statement numbers, DIMENSIØN statements, etc., as needed. The relation between the subprogram is provided through the subprogram name and/or its arguments. In Chap. 9 other methods of providing this information will be examined.

A function subprogram is a program unit that is usually employed in situations in which one set of computations leads to only one desired answer. The definition of the function is given by the function subprogram. As with the statement function, the purpose of the definition is to show what action is to be taken to arrive at the value sought.

The first statement of the function subprogram must give the name of the subprogram and the arguments in the following form:

FUNCTIØN NAME(A,B,C)

Here the name of the subprogram is NAME, and the dummy arguments are A, B, and C. In choosing the name for the function subprogram, the usual rules for naming variables must be followed. Since the function subprogram actually determines a value that is assigned to the name of the subprogram, that name must be of the type desired. In this case it is integer. Also, since the usual purpose of a function subprogram is to determine the value assigned to the subprogram name, the name should appear at least once on the left side of an arithmetic assignment statement (or be defined otherwise). Following the FUNCTIØN statement are whatever statements that are necessary to make the required computations. The last statement in a subprogram must be an END statement — used as in a main program. The RETURN statement, which usually appears as the next to last statement, signifies that execution should at this point return to the location from which the subprogram was referenced.

As an example of a complete function subprogram, assume that n pairs of numbers ($n \leq 100$) have been read into two arrays named X and Y. It is desired to compute ΣX, ΣY, $\Sigma(XY)$, and $\Sigma(YX^4)$.

(From a practical standpoint, the above values of X and Y could represent results of an experiment. With the indicated sums determined, certain statistical properties could be calculated.) A function subprogram named SUM could be written as follows to find each sum (since only one value is desired from each set of additions):

```
       FUNCTIØN SUM(J,A,B)
       DIMENSIØN A(100),B(100)
       SUM=0.
       DØ 100 K=1,J
       SUM=SUM+A(K)*B(K)
   100 CØNTINUE
       RETURN
       END
```

Note that the first statement is the FUNCTIØN statement. The name of this subprogram is SUM; thus, the value sent back will be a real value. A name of ISUM could have been used to transmit an integer value from the function subprogram. Examination of the usage of the dummy arguments in the subprogram reveals that A and B are subscripted real variables, while J is an integer single-valued variable. If a dummy argument is a subscripted variable, this variable must appear in a DIMENSIØN statement (or have its number of subscripts declared appropriately — see Chap. 9).

In a main program that utilizes the sums from the example subprogram, the method of referencing is exactly the same as for a statement function. The name of the function subprogram, SUM in this case, along with the actual arguments must be utilized in a Fortran expression. To compute the value of $\Sigma(XY)$, the following statement could be used in a program where X and Y have 100 subscripted values:

SUMXY=SUM(100,X,Y)

Once this statement is executed, the following will happen:
1) any expressions appearing as actual arguments will be evaluated;
2) actual arguments will be associated with the corresponding dummy arguments, and
3) the actions specified by the statements in the referenced function will occur.

Thus the values of subscripted arrays X and Y will be recalled from memory. The number 100 will be the value given to J in the FUNCTIØN SUM; likewise values in arrays X and Y will be given to elements in the arrays A and B, respectively. Finally, the steps indicated in FUNCTIØN SUM will be carried out (the summation of the 100 products). Notice the variable SUM appears in the function subprogram listing. When the RETURN is executed the value associated with real variable SUM is the value that will be returned to the main program and assigned to the real variable SUMXY.

Return now to the original problem statement. How can the FUNCTIØN SUM be used to compute ΣX, ΣY, and $\Sigma(XY^4)$? At first glance, it appears that it will not be possible to use FUNCTIØN SUM. This is because the subprogram is set up to sum the *products* of the elements of *two* arrays. Often programming "gimmicks" may be used to circumvent problems like this. In the main program, in order to compute the other three required sums, it is necessary to have another array, for example Ƶ, for a work array. By placing the appropriate values in the Ƶ array, the sums may be found. Observe the following:

```
      N=100
      DØ 100 J=1,N
      Ƶ(J)=1.
100   CØNTINUE
      SUMX=SUM(N,X,Ƶ)
```

If executed in a main program, the variable SUMX would contain the value ΣX. Notice that the Ƶ array is "filled" with "1."s in the DØ loop. Then the FUNCTIØN SUM is used to compute the sum of (XƵ).

The value of N is supplied to the subprogram as J in the subprogram; the value of X is transmitted as A in the subprogram; and the value of Ƶ is supplied as B. Since X and Ƶ in the main program and A and B in the subprogram have both been subscripted to the same size, the effect is to transmit the entire X and Ƶ arrays to the subprogram.

The following statement in the main program can use the subprogram to compute ΣY:

```
      SUMY=SUM(N,Y,Ƶ)
```

This time the subprogram is used, the Y array in the main program is fed into the subprogram (along with N and Ƶ as previously done).

124

Fortran

Thus when the above statement is executed, the Σ Y is computed in
FUNCTIØN SUM and transferred back to become the value of
SUMY.

Finally, in order to compute Σ (YX⁴), the Z array can be used
again to form a work array — this time consisting of values of X^4 —
as follows:

```
      DØ 101 J=1,N
      Z(J)=X(J)**4
  101 CØNTINUE
      SUMYX4=SUM(N,Y,Z)
```

The semi-complete program and the function subprogram
needed to find the four values Σ X, Σ Y, Σ (XY), Σ (YX⁴) would be
arranged as follows:

```
      DIMENSIØN X(100),Y(100),Z(100)
      READ(5,3)N
    3 FØRMAT(I5)
      READ(5,4)(X(J),Y(J),J=1,N)
    4 FØRMAT(2F10.0)
      DØ 100 J=1,N
      Z(J)=1.
  100 CØNTINUE
      SUMX=SUM(N,X,Z)
      SUMY=SUM(N,Y,Z)
      SUMXY=SUM(N,X,Y)
      DØ 101 J=1,N
      Z(J)=X(J)**4
  101 CØNTINUE
      SUMYX4=SUM(N,Y,Z)
        .
        .
        .
      STØP
      END
      FUNCTIØN SUM(J,A,B)
      DIMENSIØN A(100),B(100)
      SUM=0.
      DØ 100 K=1,J
      SUM=SUM+A(K)*B(K)
  100 CØNTINUE
```

> **RETURN**
> **END**

Since the purpose of this example is to demonstrate the use of the function subprogram, the part of the program that utilizes the computed sums has been omitted. Of course, other computations could be made with other statements. As indicated previously, the above values for X and Y could represent results of an experiment; and with the sums determined, certain statistical properties could be calculated.

A few points are worth mentioning in relation to the semi-complete program above. The function subprogram follows the END statement of the main program. Additional subprograms would follow the END statement of FUNCTIØN SUM. The order of the subprograms is not important, but all subprograms referenced within a complete Fortran program must be available at execution of the program. Remember that built-in functions are available on most compilers and do not have to be entered separately as user-designed subprograms. (If a programmer does submit a function subprogram with the same name as one of the built-in functions, the programmer's function will take precedence.)

As in the statement function, the dummy arguments of the subprogram show the manner in which values from a reference are to be used to obtain the answer sought. Also, the actual arguments in the reference must agree in order, number, and type with the dummy arguments.

Attention is also called to the fact that statement 100 appears in both the main program and the subprogram. This is perfectly acceptable since the subprogram is separate from the main program. Likewise, there is no relationship whatsoever between the variable J used in the main program and the J in the subprogram.

7-4 THE SUBRØUTINE SUBPROGRAM

Function subprograms can be used when only one value is desired from the subprogram. Actually, other values may be obtained from a function subprogram because some of the dummy arguments may be redefined in the subprogram (also, the use of the CØMMØN statement can produce the same results — see Chap. 9.). When it is necessary to compute several values in a subprogram and transmit them back to the main program, the subroutine subprogram is much more widely used.

The subroutine subprogram is similar to the function subprogram, but it has the following differences. No value is associated with the name of the subroutine. Consequently, it makes no difference which letter is used as the first one in the subroutine name. Outputs from a subroutine (that is, those values that are computed in the subroutine to be transmitted back to the main program) may be given as arguments, and there may be any number of outputs for each subroutine. (Here again, the CØMMØN statement may be used to gain additional results.) Finally, reference is made to a subroutine through use of a special statement — the CALL statement.

The definition of a subroutine is given by the subroutine subprogram. The first statement of the subroutine must give the name of the subroutine and the arguments in the following form:

SUBRØUTINE NAME(A,B,C)

In this example, the name of the subroutine is NAME, and the dummy arguments are A, B, and C. The name of a subroutine is not a variable name, and it should not be used except in its SUBRØUTINE statement and in a CALL statement. The dummy arguments have the same restrictions as for function subprograms. They usually will be either variable or array names.

Following the SUBRØUTINE statement are whatever statements are necessary to make the required computations. Generally the last statements in a subroutine will be

RETURN
END

(As in the function subprogram, the RETURN statement may be located elsewhere in the subroutine and several RETURNs are possible.)

In order to use the subroutine, a CALL statement must be employed as follows:

CALL NAME(TA,BŻ,Ż)

In this statement, the name of the subroutine referenced is NAME, and the actual arguments to transmit values to the subroutine are TA, BŻ, and Ż. These arguments may serve to provide input to the subroutine, receive results back from the subroutine, or both. If an argument is to act as input, it should be assigned a value prior to the CALL statement. Hence if TA's value is to be used in the computations in subroutine NAME, the value of TA should be specified prior to the beginning of execution of the "CALL NAME" statement. If an actual argument is to receive output from the subroutine, its corresponding dummy argument should be given a value in the subroutine prior to the execution of the subroutine's RETURN statement. Thus, in the CALL statement, if BZ̵ is to receive a value from subroutine NAME, then dummy argument B should be given a value in subroutine NAME. Whatever their specific purposes, the actual arguments in a CALL statement must agree in order, number, and type with the dummy arguments in the referenced SUBRØUTINE statement.

The execution of a CALL statement triggers the following:
1) evaluation of actual arguments that are expressions;
2) association of actual arguments with the corresponding dummy arguments; and
3) the actions specified by the "called" subroutine.

As an example of the subroutine, consider the following. Sometimes in surveying it is impossible to measure directly a certain distance because of some obstruction, such as a river. In such cases the obstructed distance can be determined indirectly using a triangle. Assume in Fig. 7-1 it is desired to determine the distances BA and

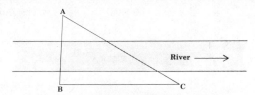

Figure 7-1

CA. A triangle ABC could be used in this situation as shown. The distance BC and angles B and C could be measured directly. The unknown distance AB can then be determined using the law of sines.

EXAMPLE 7-1

Write a computer program that will compute distances BA and CA and angle A in Fig. 7-1 if distance BC and angles B and C are known.

SOLUTION:

This is not a particularly difficult problem except for the fact that the angles would probably be measured in degrees, minutes, and (perhaps) seconds. Since the law of sines will be used to find the lengths of BA and CA, and this requires the use of function SIN, the program must convert angles measured to radians for use as actual arguments in function SIN. The conversion will be performed in a subprogram. For variety, since a subprogram to convert an angle from degrees, minutes, and seconds to radians requires only one value to be returned, a function subprogram will be used. A subroutine subprogram will be used to convert an angle in radians to degrees, minutes and seconds, since more than one value is to be returned from the subprogram.

A flow chart for preparing this program is given in Fig. 7-2, and the complete program will be as follows:

```
C
CØMMENT--READ IN MEASURED VALUES
C
        READ(5,60)BC,JBDEG,JBMIN,BSEC,JCDEG,
```

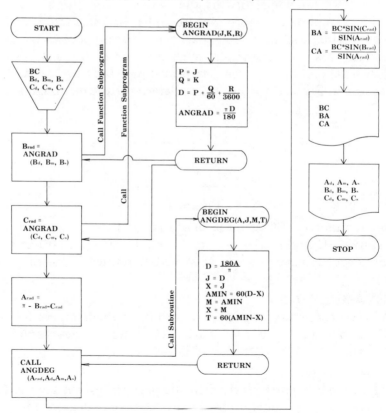

Figure 7-2 Flow Chart for Example 7-1

```
        *JCMIN,CSEC
     60 FØRMAT(F10.2,2(2I5,F6.0))
C
CØMMENT--CHANGE ANGLES FROM DEGREES, MINUTES,
C           SECONDS TO RADIANS
C
        BRAD=ANGRAD(JBDEG,JBMIN,BSEC)
        CRAD=ANGRAD(JCDEG,JCMIN,CSEC)
C
CØMMENT--SOLVE FOR ANGLE A (IN RADIANS)
C
        ARAD=3.14159265-BRAD-CRAD
C
CØMMENT--CHANGE ANGLE A FRØM RADIANS TØ
C           DEGREES, MINUTES, SECØNDS
C
        CALL ANGDEG(ARAD,JADEG,JAMIN,ASEC)
C
CØMMENT--COMPUTE LENGTHS BA AND CA USING LAW
C           ØF SINES
C
        BA=BC*SIN(CRAD)/SIN(ARAD)
        CA=BC*SIN(BRAD)/SIN(ARAD)
        WRITE(6,61)BC,BA,CA
     61 FØRMAT(13X,'RIVER PROBLEM'
       1///15X'DISTANCES'//10X,'LENGTH',7X,'FEET'
       2/12X,'BC',6X,F9.3/12X,'BA',6X,F9.3/12X,'CA',6X,
       3F9.3///17X,'ANGLES'///5X,'ANGLE DEGREES '
       4'MINUTES SECONDS')
        WRITE(6,62)JADEG,JAMIN,ASEC
     62 FØRMAT(3X,'A',5X,I3,6X,I2,5X,F4.1)
        WRITE(6,63)JBDEG,JBMIN,BSEC
     63 FØRMAT(3X,'B',5X,I3,6X,I2,5X,F4.1)
        WRITE(6,64)JCDEG,JCMIN,CSEC
     64 FØRMAT(3X,'C',5X,I3,6X,I2,5X,F4.1////
       1' ANGLES B AND C AND LENGTH BC WERE',
       2' MEASURED.'//' ANGLE A AND LENGTHS BA'
       3' AND CA WERE CALCULATED')
        STØP
        END
        FUNCTIØN ANGRAD(J,K,R)
C
CØMMENT--THIS SUBPRØGRAM CHANGES AN ANGLE
```

```
C              TØ RADIANS
C
       P=J
       Q=K
       DEGR=P+Q/60.+R/3600.
       ANGRAD=DEGR*3.14159265/180.
       RETURN
       END
       SUBRØUTINE ANGDEG(A,J,M,T)
C
CØMMENT--THIS SUBPRØGRAM CHANGES RADIANS
C              TØ DEGREES, MINUTES, SECØNDS
C
       DEGR=A*180./3.14159265
       J=DEGR
       X=J
       AMIN=(DEGR-X)*60.
       M=AMIN
       X=M
       T=(AMIN-X)*60.
       RETURN
       END
```

In the preceding program, after the input values are read, the function subprogram is used to determine the value in radians of angles B and C. Angle A is then determined, and the subroutine is referenced to convert angle A to degrees, minutes, and seconds. The law of sines is then used to compute the lengths of the two remaining sides. All important values are then printed with descriptive headings.

The function subprogram used should be self-explanatory. In this subprogram the only value computed and returned to the main program is ANGRAD, the name of the subprogram.

When the "call" is made on the subroutine ANGDEG, there are four arguments. The first of these (ARAD) has been defined prior to the CALL ANGDEG statement in the main program; hence ARAD serves as input to the subroutine. The remaining three arguments — JADEG, JAMIN, ASEC — have not been defined at the beginning of the execution of the CALL ANGDEG statement. Thus these three arguments serve to receive output from the subroutine. It should be observed that the arguments in the CALL statement agree in order, number, and type with the arguments in the first statement of the subroutine. The same is true for arguments appearing in the references to function subprogram ANGRAD and the subprogram itself.

Note that dummy argument A in the subroutine provides input to the subroutine, and accordingly appears on the right side of an arithmetic assignment statement and is in fact used to calculate another value. The other three dummy arguments — J, M, and T — are output from the subroutine, and as such, appear on the left side of an arithmetic assignment statement. The reader should study this program carefully to assure full understanding of the logic involved.

7-5 GENERAL REMARKS AND WARNINGS

In Example 7-1 the need for a subroutine to convert an angle from radians to degrees, minutes, and seconds is not great, since the subroutine is called only once from the main program. In this case the statements in the subroutine could have easily been placed in the main program itself. The value of the subroutine might be more obvious if additional calls on it had been made from different locations in the main program. In complex programs it is common to employ numerous subroutines, each of which does a part of the overall problem. A main program could then be used with appropriate calls on the subroutines as needed. A large number of "canned" subroutines are available that can be effectively used in this way.

Certain ideas that are applicable to both function and subroutine subprograms are given next. Subprograms were shown to be referenced from main programs in examples in this chapter. Subprograms may also reference other subprograms. A statement function may have a function subprogram included in its definition expression. In any case, all referenced subprograms must be included as user-specified or as compiler-specified subprograms.

Obviously, a subroutine could be written to accomplish anything for which a function subprogram is designed. Likewise a function subprogram could be written to accomplish anything for which a statement function is designed. Thus a programmer must consider the nature of the three concepts described in this chapter in deciding when each is best employed. If one expression is to be evaluated in only one program and only one value desired, then a statement function is most efficient. If one value is desired, but more than one step is required in obtaining that value, then a function subprogram is appropriate. For all other cases a subroutine is best — i.e., usually situations in which more than one value is required from a set of computations. Some programmers use only subroutines when subprograms are needed.

Finally, three warnings will be given. First, the name of a subprogram is a name that is special to a program. It is not a variable name and should not be assigned a value except for a function name — and then only in the function subprogram itself.

Next, a subprogram *may never reference itself* — either directly or indirectly. This can be a matter of concern for large programs in which subprograms contain references to other subprograms.

The last warning is a special situation in a subprogram reference. If an actual argument is a constant, the dummy argument in the reference subprogram may never appear on the left side of an assignment statement or be otherwise changed. For example, consider the following:

CALL SUB(A,100,D)

The second actual argument is 100. It is obviously intended to be an input value. In the SUBRØUTINE statement:

SUBRØUTINE SUB(X,K,Ƶ)

K is the dummy argument designed to receive the constant 100 as input and use that input. Therefore, K would probably only be used on the right side of an arithmetic assignment statement. K should not appear on the left side of an assignment statement or be redefined in any way.

Chapter 9 contains topics, among others, that are directly related to the concepts of this chapter. However, the coverage in this chapter is aimed at the most frequently encountered usages of statement function and subprograms.

7-6 PROBLEMS

7-1   Define the statement function to find the "positive root solution" of a quadratic equation, $ax^2+bx+c=0$, as determined by:

$$x = \frac{-b \pm \sqrt{b^2-4ac}}{2a}$$

7-2   Use the statement function from Problem 7-1 to solve the following equation for x:

   $2X^2-13X+3=0$

Show the necessary Fortran coding to solve for X.

7-3   Same as Problem 7-2 using the equation:
$-5X^2+2X+15=0$

7-4   Write a function subprogram to compute Y as a function of X as defined by:
$Y(x) = 10X+3.56$ if $X<0$
$Y(x) = 13.2$ if $X=0$
$Y(x) = (X+2)^{0.5}$ if $X>0$

7-5   Using the function subprogram of Problem 7-4, write the 4 statements necessary to evaluate:
(a) A=Y(3π+2)
(b) A=Y(4.0)
(c) C=[Y(2)+13]/[Y(-1+A)]
(d) D=Y(E)

In Problems 7-6 through 7-10, find the error, if any, in each statement or group of statements.

7-6   **SUBRUTINE NAME(A)**

7-7   **FUNCTIØN(A,B,C)**

7-8   **CALL SUBRØUTINE ØNE(X,Y)**

7-9   **CALC(A,B)=(2.*A+4.*B)/2.3**

      |
      |
      |
Z=CALC(2*I,J)

7-10 **FUNCTIØN ØNE(X,Y,Z̶)**

      |
      |
      |
STØP
END

7-11 a) Write a subprogram to find the transpose of a 3 by 3 matrix:
$$\begin{vmatrix} 5 & 3 & 2 \\ 6 & 1 & 8 \\ 9 & 7 & 4 \end{vmatrix}$$

      b) Extend the results of part (a) to produce a subprogram capable of providing the transpose of a matrix with m rows and n columns.

7-12 Using the same matrix as in Problem 7-11, write a subprogram to find the matrix's determinant.

7-13 Write a statement function to compute the value of the sine of x radians by the first five terms of the series:

$$\sin x = x - \frac{x^3}{3!} + \frac{x^5}{5!} - \frac{x^7}{7!} + \frac{x^9}{9!} - \ \ldots\ldots$$

7-14 Give the statements necessary to compare the value from Problem 7-13 with the value obtained from the built-in function SIN for an angle of 85°.

7-15 Repeat Problem 7-13, using a function subprogram capable of including N terms from the series in sin x.

7-16 Given:

A main program
```
      I=1
      TX=1.
      SX=3.
      RX=5.
      PX=7.
      CALL SUB(I,TX,SX,RX,PX)
  110 CØNTINUE
        |
        |
        |
      END
```

A subprogram
```
      SUBRØUTINE SUB(N,W,X,Y,Z)
      DØ 10 I=1,N
   10 W=W+X+Y+Z
      RETURN
      END
```

Find: When statement 110 is executed, what would be the values of I, TX, RX, and PX?

7-17 Give the Fortran coding necessary to have a main program read ten values into an array; then have a subprogram find the largest value and print it.

7-18 Write a function subprogram that will calculate the value of n!, where n! = 1×2×3×4×...×n.

7-19 Using the subprogram from Problem 7-18, write a main program to evaluate the combinations of n things, taken r at a time:

$$C_{nr} = \frac{n!}{r!(n-r)!}$$

(This is also the binomial coefficient.)

7-20 Write a *complete* program to evaluate:

$$Y = \tan^{-1} (.3882) + 2.$$

and

$$Z = \left[\tan^{-1} (1.56)\right]^2$$

In evaluating Y and Z, develop a function subprogram to calculate $\tan^{-1}$ based on the following series:

$$\tan^{-1} x = x - (x^3/3) + (x^5/5) - (x^7/7) + \ldots \qquad \text{if } x < 1$$

$$\tan^{-1} x = (\pi/2) - (1/x) + \frac{1}{(3x^3)} - \frac{1}{(5x^5)} + \frac{1}{(7x^7)} - \ldots \quad \text{if } x > 1$$

Use 10 terms of each series in your subprogram.

7-21 The equation of a least squares regression line is: $Y = a_0 + a_1 X$, where

$$a_0 = \frac{(\Sigma Y)[\Sigma(X^2)] - (\Sigma X)[\Sigma(XY)]}{N\Sigma(X^2) - (\Sigma X)^2}$$

$$a_1 = \frac{N\Sigma(XY) - (\Sigma X)(\Sigma Y)}{N\Sigma(X^2) - (\Sigma X)^2}$$

and N = number of observations
    X = independent variable values
    Y = dependent variable values

Using the logic of the example of Sec. 7-3, write a function subprogram to solve for the summations; then evaluate a_0 and a_1 in a main program.

7-22 Use the subprogram of Problem 7-21 to find the least squares coefficients for the following observed data:

OBSERVATION #	1	2	3	4	5	6	7	8	9	10
X	6	8	10	12	14	16	18	20	22	24
Y	3.8	3.7	4.0	3.9	4.3	4.2	4.2	4.4	4.5	4.5

Have the program print the least squares equation.

7-23 In Problem 7-1, a statement function was desired which evaluated the "positive root solution" of a quadratic function. Revise the statement function written for Problem 7-1 to include a factor that will allow the execution of a statement function to produce either the "positive root solution" *or* the "negative root solution"; i.e., devise *one* statement to determine both roots of a quadratic equation as given by:

$$x = \left[-b \pm (b^2 - 4ac)^{0.5}\right] / [2a]$$

8
Applications

Although a number of applications, or example programs, have been presented in the first seven chapters, almost all of them were limited in scope and were designed mainly to illustrate a specific programming technique. The purpose of Chap. 8 is to show how the various programming techniques already presented can be used collectively for a very few of the enormous number of possible engineering applications. The reader will note that no new programming techniques are introduced in this chapter.

8-1 PRINT PLOTTING

One important aspect of most engineers' work is to display data in graphical form to facilitate visualization and presentation. There are available commercial plotters that can be used with computers to plot graphs; however, these are generally expensive and may not be readily available when needed. Thus, it is the intention herein to show how regular Fortran programming can be used to plot graphs using the computer.

Suppose it is desired to plot a graph of y as a function of x according to the following:

if $1 < x \leq 10$	$y = 2x + 2$
if $10 < x \leq 30$	$y = -0.3x^2 + 15x - 102$
if $30 < x \leq 40$	$y = -x + 112$

Clearly the first part and the last part of this graph are straight lines while the middle part of the graph is a parabola. There are several ways of approaching this problem.

One method is to compute each data point and write out the graph one line at the time. In order to do this, a (single) subscripted variable of size 101 will be used. The first step will be to write out a line of dots (decimal points), which will actually be the y axis of the graph. (Using this method, the graph will be printed sideways, but a piece of paper can always be rotated.) Hence, the first several statements in the program would be:

```
      DIMENSIØN GRAPH(101)
      DATA DØT/'.'/
      DØ 100 J=1,101
      GRAPH(J)=DØT
  100 CØNTINUE
      WRITE(6,99)GRAPH
   99 FØRMAT('1',101A1)
```

In this program segment, the first statement, of course, establishes GRAPH as a subscripted variable of size 101 spaces. (Some machines will require the use of an integer variable when used in this context.) The DØ loop assigns the value of a decimal point (a "dot") to each element in the array GRAPH. The next two statements then write out these 101 dots in a single line. Note that no subscript appears on the subscripted variable GRAPH in the WRITE statement; hence the entire array is written out. In the FØRMAT designation '1', the 1 causes this line of output to be at the top of the page (Why?). The first dot will represent the x axis. The 101A1 in the FØRMAT allows for 101 values (in this case the 101 values of the array GRAPH) to be written out in A1 FØRMAT. Thus the net effect of executing this statement is to write out 101 dots in a single row at the top of a page. The first dot, which represents the x axis, represents the plotting position for a value of y equal to zero. The second dot represents the plotting position for a value of y equal to one. Thus 101 positions are required to plot values up to y equal to 100.

When the next line of output is written, it is desired to again place a decimal point at the left side of the page to represent the x axis of the graph. This is done by the statement GRAPH(1)=DØT in the program segment that follows. Since this line of output will actually write out the line of the graph for x equal to 1, a plotting symbol (e.g., an asterisk) representing the data point is needed at the appropriate place with respect to the y axis. The rest of the line should be blanks. The next statements would be:

```
      DATA STAR/'*'/,BLANK/' '/
      DØ 101 J=1,101
      GRAPH(J)=BLANK
  101 CØNTINUE
      Y=2.*1.+2.
      JY=Y+0.5+1.0
```

```
      GRAPH(1)=DØT
      GRAPH(JY)=STAR
      WRITE(6,98)GRAPH
   98 FØRMAT(1X,101A1)
```

In this program segment, the DØ loop replaces all of the dots in the array GRAPH by blanks. Then the value of Y is computed for X=1. (giving in this case Y=4.). Since it is desired to place a plotting symbol on the line at the appropriate place with respect to the y axis, it is necessary to determine the "integer value" of Y (the statement JY=Y+0.5+1.0) and use it as the subscript to place the asterisk in the appropriate place on the array GRAPH (the statement GRAPH(JY)=STAR). In the statement JY=Y+0.5+1.0, the value of 0.5 is added to Y prior to truncating to get the closest integer for the value of JY. The value of 1.0 is added in order to allow the first point to represent zero. (JY could be assigned the sum Y+1.5) Once this is done, it is only necessary to write out the array again. This corresponds to the line on the graph where X=1. and consists of a dot in the first column, an asterisk in column 5 (corresponding to Y=4, as was computed for X=1.) and the rest blank.

Once this step is accomplished, the procedure can be repeated for the next line on the graph (i.e., X=2.). There is a little bookkeeping necessary, however. The asterisk in column 5 needs to be replaced with a blank. Hence

GRAPH(JY)=BLANK

Now the procedure can be repeated for X equal to 2. It is much easier, however, to revise the procedure slightly and incorporate everything into a DØ loop.

```
      DØ 102 K=1,40
      X=K
      GRAPH(1)=DØT
      IF(X.LE.10.)Y=2.*X+2.
      IF(X.GT.10..AND.X.LE.30.)Y=-0.3*X**2+15.*X-102.
      IF(X.GT.30.)Y=-X+112.
      JY=Y+0.5+1.0
      GRAPH(JY)=STAR
      WRITE(6,98)GRAPH
   98 FØRMAT(1X,101A1)
      GRAPH(JY)=BLANK
```

```
    102 CØNTINUE
```

In this DØ loop, note that X is set equal to the index K. Thus X, like K, varies from 1 to 40. Note the use of logical IF statements to determine the value of Y corresponding to any value of X.

Actually, when this DØ loop is satisfied, the graph has been written out, and the stated problem completed. Hence the entire program would be:

```
      DIMENSIØN GRAPH(101)
      DATA DØT/'.'/,STAR/'*'/,BLANK/' '/
      DØ 100 J=1,101
      GRAPH(J)=DØT
  100 CØNTINUE
      WRITE(6,99)GRAPH
   99 FØRMAT('1',101A1)
      DØ 101 J=1,101
      GRAPH(J)=BLANK
  101 CØNTINUE
      DØ 102 K=1,40
      X=K
      GRAPH(1)=DØT
      IF(X.LE.10.)Y=2.*X+2.
      IF(X.GT.10..AND.X.LE.30.)Y=-.3*X**2+15.*X-102.
      IF(X.GT.30.)Y=-X+112.
      JY=Y+0.5+1.0
      GRAPH(JY)=STAR
      WRITE(6,98)GRAPH
   98 FØRMAT(1X,101A1)
      GRAPH(JY)=BLANK
  102 CØNTINUE
      STØP
      END
```

Figure 8-1 shows the output from running the above program. The arrow indicates the direction the paper came off the printer.

It will be noted that this graph is somewhat crude. There are no labels, numerical markings, or indications of units along the axes. It is, however, a good qualitative representation of the data, and more elaborate programming steps could be added to improve the graph. It might also be noted that all values of X and Y were positive numbers within the range of 1 to 100. If negative numbers

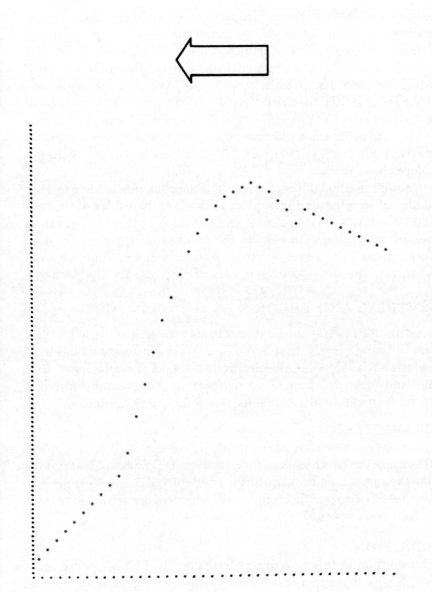

Figure 8-1 Output From Graphing Program

are involved, requiring the shifting of axes, or if very large (or very small) numbers are involved, requiring the use of a "scale factor," then more sophisticated programming will be required. For example, if values of Y ranged from -50 to +50 in the example above, the program could be modified by changing the statement GRAPH(1)=DØT to GRAPH(51)=DØT and the statement JY=Y+0.5+1.0 to JY=Y+0.5+51.0. Or, if values of Y ranged from zero to 1000, the program could be modified by changing the statement JY=Y+0.5+1.0 to JY=Y/10.0+0.5+1.0. It will be left to the reader to explore these further.

Another method of programming this problem would be to use a double subscripted variable, place dots along two sides of the (two dimensional) array to represent the axes, place asterisks at appropriate places with respect to the axes to represent the data points, place blanks everywhere else, and then write out the array one row at the time. This is left as an exercise for the reader.

8-2 TRIAL AND ERROR

Sometimes the most expedient way to solve an engineering problem is by trial and error — that is, continue trying different values until a solution that satisfies all conditions is found. Usually, however, a trial and error solution is carried out in a systematic manner, rather than randomly. Consider the following example:

EXAMPLE 8-1

For a rectangular channel of width w, slope s, and "n" value n, determine the depth of flow for a particular flow rate. That is, for these channel conditions, what is the depth of flow in feet necessary to allow a specified number of cubic feet per second of water to flow each second?

SOLUTION:

The solution of this program is based on the Manning formula, which was presented in Chap. 4. That formula is

$$V = \frac{1.486}{n} R^{2/3} s^{1/2}$$

This equation evaluates the average velocity (V), whereas this example problem is concerned with flow rate. Since flow rate (Q) is equal to area multiplied by velocity, the equation above can be modified to become

$$Q = A \left(\frac{1.486}{n}\right) R^{2/3} s^{1/2}$$

Substituting for A and R gives

$$Q = wd \left(\frac{1.486}{n}\right) \left(\frac{wd}{w+2d}\right)^{2/3} s^{1/2}$$

This equation is not amenable to a direct solution for d. Hence, a trial and error solution may be in order. The equation above may be rearranged to become

$$Q - wd \left(\frac{1.486}{n}\right) \left(\frac{wd}{w+2d}\right)^{2/3} s^{1/2} = 0$$

Since the value of d must be a positive value, one could substitute different positive values of d (along with the other given values of Q, w, n, and s) until one is found that makes the left side of the equation equal to zero. There are two pitfalls here, however. One is that a random selection of values of d could require a large number of "guesses" and a lot of luck to find the right answer. The other is that it would be difficult to find a value of d that would cause the left side of the equation to be exactly zero — that is, to the 8 or so places beyond the decimal as computed by the computer. An alternative would be to select a very small value of d, for example 0.1, and substitute this value into the equation to compute the value of the left side of the equation. Almost certainly this small value of d will not be the solution — that is, the one to make the left side of the equation equal to zero. The value of d can then be incremented by a certain amount, for example 0.1, and this value substituted into the equation. In all likelihood if successive values of d are substituted into the equation, the successive values of the left side of the equation will get closer to zero and will eventually "pass through zero," change sign, and then move away from zero. Hence, the procedure used in the program that follows is to substitute successive values of d into the equation until a sign change is encountered in the value of the left side of the equation. The actual value of d can then be approximated by simple ratio.

A flow-chart for this problem is given in Fig. 8-2, and the program is given below.

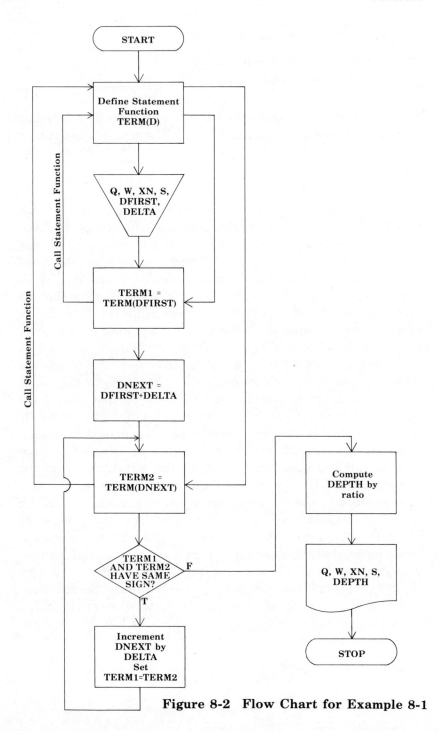

Figure 8-2 Flow Chart for Example 8-1

```
C
COMMENT--DEFINE STATEMENT FUNCTION TO COMPUTE
C           LEFT SIDE OF EQUATION
C
          TERM(D)=Q-W*D*1.486/XN*(W*D/(W+2.*D))
         1**(2./3.)*SQRT(S)
C
COMMENT--READ INPUT DATA
C
          READ(5,900)Q,W,XN,S,DFIRST,DELTA
      900 FORMAT(6F10.0)
C
COMMENT--SOLVE FOR LEFT SIDE FOR DFIRST
C
          TERM1=TERM(DFIRST)
C
COMMENT--INCREMENT DFIRST BY DELTA
C           AND SOLVE FOR LEFT SIDE
C
          DNEXT=DFIRST+DELTA
       22 TERM2=TERM(DNEXT)
C
COMMENT--CHECK TO SEE IF TERM1 AND TERM2 HAVE
C           THE SAME SIGN. IF THEY DO, INCREMENT
C           DNEXT, SET TERM1=TERM2, AND RETURN TO
C           COMPUTE NEW VALUE OF TERM2.
C
C           IF THEY DO NOT, COMPUTE DEPTH BY RATIO
C           BETWEEN DFIRST AND DNEXT.
C
          IF(TERM1*TERM2)20,20,21
       21 DNEXT=DNEXT+DELTA
          TERM1=TERM2
          GO TO 22
       20 DEPTH=DNEXT-ABS(TERM2)*DELTA/
         *        (ABS(TERM1)+ABS(TERM2))
C
COMMENT--WRITE RESULTS
C
          WRITE(6,800)W,XN,S,Q,DEPTH
      800 FORMAT(1X,'FOR A RECTANGULAR CHANNEL '
         1 ,F6.0,' FT WIDE, MANNING N VALUE OF ',F6.3,
         2', SLOPE OF ',F8.6,', AND FLOW RATE OF ',F6.0,
```

```
      3' CFS,'//1X,'THE DEPTH WILL BE ',F6.1,' FT.')
      STØP
      END
```

It will be noted that the program above is set up so that an initial depth and an increment are read initially. One might, for example, set both an initial depth and an increment of 0.1 ft. Suppose a specific application of the program using these values gives a depth of 12.16 ft. This is, of course, an approximate answer; a more accurate answer might be obtained by rerunning the program using an initial depth of 12.0 and an increment of 0.01. This should result in a more accurate answer.

The procedure used in the program written for Example 8-1 might be described as using "brute force." It might not even work in this and other similar situations, and a more sophisticated method (for example, the Newton-Raphson method) may be required; but sometimes one can use a brute force method, such as trial and error, more expeditiously than taking the time to perfect a more sophisticated method.

8-3 ITERATIVE SOLUTIONS

The trial and error solution presented in the last section actually involved an iterative procedure, but no highly sophisticated, analytical procedure was used to arrive at a solution. As indicated previously, that solution was obtained mostly by "brute force." The iterative solutions alluded to in this chapter refer to ones that utilize sophisticated, analytical procedures to arrive at a solution. There are many such numerical methods available, and the reader is referred to one of the many books available on numerical methods. Iterative procedures are particularly amenable to computer solutions.

Suppose it is necessary to solve the following equation:

$$x^3 - 25x^2 + 60x + 39 = 0$$

There are several iterative types of solutions that can be used to solve for the three roots of this equation. One method is to modify the equation so that x stands alone on one side of the equation. Doing this gives

$$x = 25 - \frac{60}{x} - \frac{39}{x^2} = F(x)$$

One can then assume a value of x and substitute that value into the right side of the equation, giving F(x). If the computed value of F(x) is equal (or nearly equal) to the assumed value of x, then that value of x is one of the roots of the equation. If the computed value of F(x) is not equal to the assumed value of x, a new value of x equal to F(x) may be substituted into the equation, giving a new value of F(x). If the new value of F(x) is equal (or nearly equal) to the old value of F(x), then that value of F(x) is one of the roots of the equation. This procedure can be repeated until a solution is found. As will be noted later, this procedure may not yield a solution under some circumstances.

To illustrate, assume a value of x of 22 to be a root of the equation above. Substituting this value of x into the equation gives

$$25 - \frac{60}{22} - \frac{39}{(22)^2} = 22.19 = F(x)$$

Since the computed value of F(x) of 22.19 is not equal to the assumed value of x of 22, a new value of x equal to F(x) of 22.19 will be substituted into the equation giving

$$25 - \frac{60}{22.19} - \frac{39}{(22.19)^2} = 22.22 = F(x)$$

Again, a new value of x equal to 22.22 may be substituted into the equation giving

$$25 - \frac{60}{22.22} - \frac{39}{(22.22)^2} = 22.22 = F(x)$$

Thus, one solution of the equation is x equal to 22.22 (to two decimal places).

In order for this method to work properly, the initial assumed value of x must be reasonably close to the correct value. Appropriate initial assumed values of x may be obtained by preparing a table of values of x and corresponding values obtained by substituting x values into the original equation. Such a table for the equation above would be

x	value of left side of original equation
-2	-189
-1	-47
0	39
1	75
2	67

3	21
4	-57
5	-161
6	-285
7	-423
8	-569
9	-717
10	-861
11	-995
12	-1113
13	-1209
14	-1277
15	-1311
16	-1305
17	-1253
18	-1149
19	-987
20	-761
21	-465
22	-93
23	361
24	903

As mentioned in the previous section, a solution to the equation should occur near where there is a sign change in successive values of the left side of the equation. One notes in the table above that a solution should be found between x equal to -1 and x equal to zero, between x equal to 3 and x equal to 4, and between x equal to 22 and x equal to 23. This is how the initial assumed value of x of 22 in the illustration was determined.

EXAMPLE 8-2

Prepare a program that will solve an equation by the method just described. The program must work for any number (up to some reasonable limit) of terms (and exponents of x) in the equation.

SOLUTION:

A flow chart for this problem is given in Fig. 8-3, and the program is given below.

        DIMENSIØN X(100)
  C

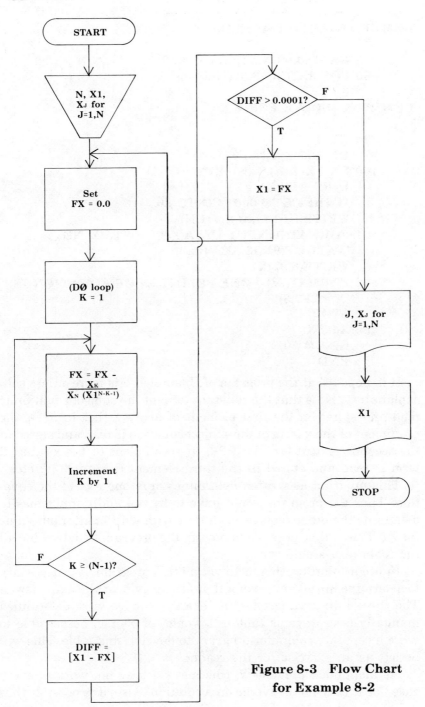

**Figure 8-3   Flow Chart
for Example 8-2**

```
CØMMENT--READ INPUT DATA
C
        READ(5,90)N,X1,(X(J),J=1,N)
     90 FØRMAT(I5,F8.0/(10F8.0))
C
CØMMENT--SØLVE FØR F(X)
C
     70 FX=0.
        DØ 100 K=1,N-1
    100 FX=FX-X(K)/X(N)/X1**(N-K-1)
        DIFF=ABS(X1-FX)
        IF(DIFF.GT.0.0001)GØ TØ 80
        WRITE(6,91)(J,X(J),J=1,N)
     91 FØRMAT('1INPUT DATA'//'       TERM NØ.
       1'VALUE'/(8X,I3,3X,F10.2))
        WRITE(6,92)X1
     92 FØRMAT(//'    ØNE SØLUTIØN ØF EQUATIØN IS '
       *'X = ',F7.3)
        STØP
     80 X1=FX
        GØ TØ 70
        END
```

It is hoped that the program of Example 8-2 is more or less self-explanatory. Note that the constant term of the subject equation is read and stored in the first element of array X [i.e., in X(1)]; the coefficient of the x term of the subject equation is read and stored in the second element [i.e., in X(2)]; the coefficient of the x-squared term is read and stored in the third element [i.e., in X(3)]; etc.

This program as written determines only one root of the equation. Thus the program would have to be run additional times to determine the other roots — each time with a different input value for X1. It would be possible to modify the program to determine all the roots in a single run.

In order to utilize this method and this program, it is necessary to determine initial values of x that are fairly near the real answer. The three initial values for the example above were determined manually (see previous table). It would, of course, be possible to write a separate computer program to develop this table. This will be left as an exercise for the reader.

As mentioned previously, this method may not work in every case, for it may not converge on a solution. Also, it is possible that some or all of the roots of a particular equation may be imaginary and therefore not obtainable by this method. In any event, a certain amount of personal judgment is necessary both in determining the initial values to use and in applying the method.

8-4 MATRIX MANIPULATIONS

In Chap. 6 the double subscripted variable was introduced. Quite obviously, a double subscripted variable can be conveniently thought of as representing a two-dimensional matrix. Certain engineering problems can be handled with ease by utilizing matrices.

Three basic matrix operations are addition, subtraction, and multiplication. Matrix addition is done by adding each term of one matrix to the respective corresponding term of another matrix. In order to be added together, two (or more) matrices must have an equal number of rows and an equal number of columns. Matrix addition can be expressed in equation form as

$$d_{i,j} = e_{i,j} + f_{i,j}$$

where $d_{i,j}$ represents an element of the array that is the sum of the arrays and $e_{i,j}$ and $f_{i,j}$ represent elements of the arrays to be added.

A simple illustration of the addition of two arrays follows:

$$|E| = \begin{vmatrix} 6 & 2 \\ -1 & 5 \end{vmatrix} \qquad |F| = \begin{vmatrix} 5 & 0 \\ 9 & 2 \end{vmatrix}$$

$$|D| = |E| + |F| = \begin{vmatrix} 6+5 & 2+0 \\ -1+9 & 5+2 \end{vmatrix} = \begin{vmatrix} 11 & 2 \\ 8 & 7 \end{vmatrix}$$

Matrix subtraction is essentially the same as addition except that the respective terms are subtracted. Thus the equation for matrix subtraction would be

$$d_{i,j} = e_{i,j} - f_{i,j}$$

Matrix multiplication is somewhat more complicated than addition or subtraction. Each term $d_{i,j}$ in the matrix that is the product of two matrices is obtained by multiplying each term in the ith row of the first matrix being multiplied by the terms in the jth column of the second matrix and adding the products. In order to multiply two matrices $|E|$ $|F|$ in that order, the number of columns in $|E|$ must be equal to the number of rows in $|F|$. Matrix multiplication can be expressed in equation form as

$$d_{i,k} = \sum_{j=1}^{n} e_{i,j} f_{j,k}$$

where n is the number of columns in $|E|$, which must be equal to the number of rows in $|F|$.

An illustration of matrix multiplication follows:

$$|E| = \begin{vmatrix} 3 & 6 \\ 9 & 2 \end{vmatrix} \qquad |F| = \begin{vmatrix} 5 & 1 & 0 & 6 \\ 2 & 0 & 4 & 8 \end{vmatrix}$$

$$|D| = |E||F| = \begin{vmatrix} 3(5)+6(2) & 3(1)+6(0) & 3(0)+6(4) & 3(6)+6(8) \\ 9(5)+2(2) & 9(1)+2(0) & 9(0)+2(4) & 9(6)+2(8) \end{vmatrix}$$

$$= \begin{vmatrix} 27 & 3 & 24 & 66 \\ 49 & 9 & 8 & 70 \end{vmatrix}$$

It should be pointed out that, in matrix multiplication, the product of $|A|$ $|B|$ is not in general equal to the product of $|B|$ $|A|$.

Example 8-3, which follows, illustrates Fortran programming of addition, subtraction, and multiplication of matrices. Another common matrix operation, matrix inversion, will not be covered here; however, a number of "canned" subroutines are available for performing matrix inversion.

EXAMPLE 8-3

Prepare a program that will read two matrices by rows and then add, subtract, and multiply the two matrices. Include an initial data card that tells how many columns and rows each matrix has. Use subroutines for the addition, subtraction, and multiplication.

SOLUTION:

A flow chart for this problem is given in Fig. 8-4, and the program is given below:

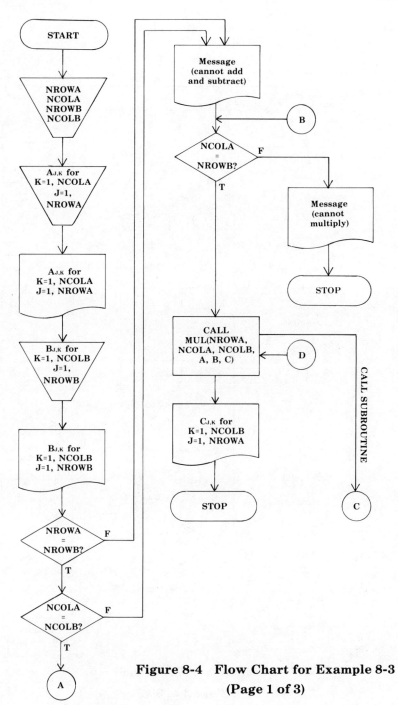

Figure 8-4 Flow Chart for Example 8-3
(Page 1 of 3)

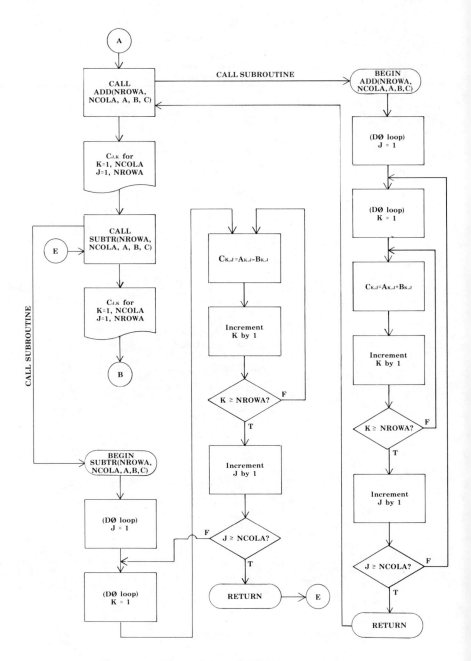

Figure 8-4 (Continued)

(Page 2 of 3)

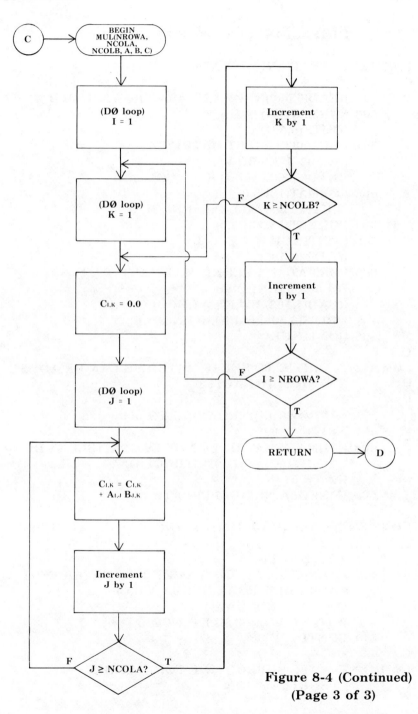

Figure 8-4 (Continued)
(Page 3 of 3)

```
          DIMENSIØN  A(100,100),B(100,100),C(100,100)
C
CØMMENT--READ INPUT DATA
C
          READ(5,500)NRØWA,NCØLA,NRØWB,NCØLB
      500 FØRMAT(4I4)
          WRITE(6,501)
      501 FØRMAT('1 FIRST MATRIX' /)
          DØ 502 J=1,NRØWA
          READ(5,503)(A(J,K),K=1,NCØLA)
      503 FØRMAT(16F5.0)
          WRITE(6,504)(A(J,K),K=1,NCØLA)
      504 FØRMAT(1X,25F5.0)
      502 CØNTINUE
          WRITE(6,505)
      505 FØRMAT(//' SECØND MATRIX'/)
          DØ 506 J=1,NRØWB
          READ(5,503)(B(J,K),K=1,NCØLB)
          WRITE(6,504)(B(J,K),K=1,NCØLB)
      506 CØNTINUE
C
CØMMENT--CHECK TØ SEE IF MATRICES CAN BE ADDED
C          AND SUBTRACTED
C
          IF(NRØWA.EQ.NRØWB)GØ TØ 509
      507 WRITE(6,508)
      508 FØRMAT(' MATRICES NØT CØMPATIBLE FØR'
         *' ADDITION AND SUBTRACTION'/)
          GØ TØ 514
      509 IF(NCØLA.NE.NCØLB)GØ TØ 507
C
CØMMENT--CALL SUBRØUTINE FØR MATRIX ADDITIØN
C
          WRITE(6,510)
      510 FØRMAT(///' ADDITIØN ØF THE MATRICES'/)
          CALL ADD(NRØWA,NCØLA,A,B,C)
          DØ 511 J=1,NRØWA
          WRITE(6,504)(C(J,K),K=1,NCØLA)
      511 CØNTINUE
C
CØMMENT--CALL SUBRØUTINE FØR MATRIX
C          SUBTRACTIØN
C
```

```
      WRITE(6,512)
  512 FØRMAT(///' SUBTRACTIØN ØF THE'
     *' MATRICES'/)
      CALL SUBTR(NRØWA,NCØLA,A,B,C)
      DØ 513 J=1,NRØWA
      WRITE(6,504)(C(J,K),K=1,NCØLA)
  513 CØNTINUE
C
CØMMENT--CHECK TØ SEE IF MATRICES CAN BE
C         MULTIPLIED
C
  514 IF(NCØLA.EQ.NRØWB)GØ TØ 517
      WRITE(6,516)
  516 FØRMAT(' MATRICES NØT CØMPATIBLE FØR'
     *' MULTIPLICATION')
      STØP
C
CØMMENT--CALL SUBRØUTINE FØR MATRIX
C         MULTIPLICATIØN
C
  517 WRITE(6,518)
  518 FØRMAT(///' MULTIPLICATIØN ØF THE'
     *' MATRICES'/)
      CALL MUL(NRØWA,NCØLA,NCØLB,A,B,C)
      DØ 519 J=1,NRØWA
      WRITE(6,504)(C(J,K),K=1,NCØLB)
  519 CØNTINUE
      STØP
      END
      SUBRØUTINE ADD(NRØWA,NCØLA,A,B,C)
      DIMENSIØN A(100,100),B(100,100),C(100,100)
      DØ 500 J=1,NCØLA
      DØ 500 K=1,NRØWA
      C(K,J)=A(K,J)+B(K,J)
  500 CØNTINUE
      RETURN
      END
      SUBRØUTINE SUBTR(NRØWA,NCØLA,A,B,C)
      DIMENSIØN A(100,100),B(100,100),C(100,100)
      DØ 500 J=1,NCØLA
      DØ 500 K=1,NRØWA
      C(K,J)=A(K,J)-B(K,J)
  500 CØNTINUE
```

```
        RETURN
        END
        SUBRØUTINE MUL(NRØWA,NCØLA,NCØLB,A,B,C)
        DIMENSIØN A(100,100),B(100,100),C(100,100)
        DØ 500 I=1,NRØWA
        DØ 500 K=1,NCØLB
        C(I,K)=0.0
        DØ 600 J=1,NCØLA
        C(I,K)=C(I,K)+A(I,J)*B(J,K)
    600 CØNTINUE
    500 CØNTINUE
        RETURN
        END
```

The program written for Example 8-3 illustrates the addition, subtraction, and multiplication of two matrices, but it is somewhat incongruous in applicability. In order to use the program to add (or subtract) two matrices, the matrices must have an equal number of rows and an equal number of columns. In order to use it to multiply two matrices, the number of columns in the first matrix must be equal to the number of rows in the second matrix. The reader will note that certain tests have been built into this program to determine (1) if the two matrices read are compatible for addition and subtraction and (2) if they are compatible for multiplication. Thus, depending upon the relative sizes of the two matrices read when this program is executed, the program may either (1) add, subtract, and multiply the two matrices, (2) only add and subtract them, (3) only multiply them, or (4) neither add and subtract nor multiply them. One will note that the matrices will be added, subtracted, and multiplied only in the case of two square matrices with an equal number of rows and columns.

8-5 STATISTICAL ANALYSES

Engineers often find it necessary to analyze experimental data statistically and also to display the results in convenient form (such as graphically). There are many, many methods of statistical analysis, and obviously extensive study of these is far beyond the scope of this book. For illustrative purposes, one relatively simple method of statistical analysis, linear regression, is presented in the following example.

EXAMPLE 8-4

Often experimental data are obtained that consist of values of one parameter and corresponding values of a dependent parameter. In analyzing such data, it may be helpful to find the equation of the "best straight line" that fits the experimental data. This is known as "linear regression" and is based on least squares analysis. The procedure was outlined in Problem 7-21. Prepare a program that reads a number of x, y pairs of data and computes the best straight line that fits these data. Then have the computer plot both the original data points and the straight line on a simple graph.

SOLUTION:

As indicated above, the procedure for determining the best straight line was outlined in Problem 7-21. Since this method requires the computation of several sums, the function subprogram given in Sec. 7-3 will be used here. Finally, the general techniques outlined in Sec. 8-1 will be utilized to present the results graphically. A double subscripted variable will be used. Assume an initial data card will be included that will tell how many x, y pairs are to be read.

A flow chart for this problem is given in Fig. 8-5, and a program follows:

```
      DIMENSIØN X(101),Y(101),Z(101),GRAPH(101,101)
C
CØMMENT--READ INPUT DATA
C
      DATA BLANK,DØT,STAR/' ','.','*'/
      READ(5,997)N
  997 FØRMAT(I4)
      READ(5,998)(X(J),Y(J),J=1,N)
  998 FØRMAT(2F10.0)
      XN=N
      DØ 1000 J=1,N
 1000 Z(J)=1.0
C
CØMMENT--USE FUNCTIØN SUBPRØGRAM TØ CØMPUTE
C        SUMS OF XY, X**2, X, Y
C
      SUMXY=SUM(N,X,Y)
      SUMXX=SUM(N,X,X)
      SUMX=SUM(N,X,Z)
```

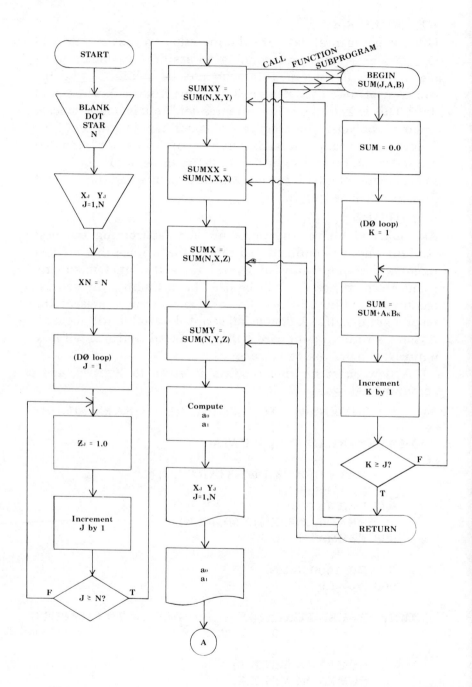

Figure 8-5   Flow Chart for Example 8-4   (Page 1 of 3)

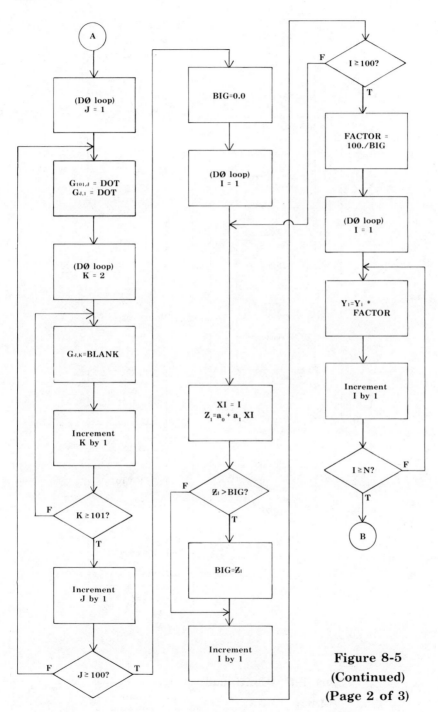

**Figure 8-5
(Continued)
(Page 2 of 3)**

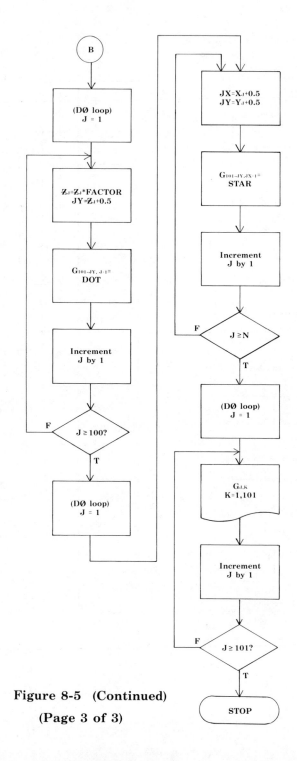

Figure 8-5 (Continued)

(Page 3 of 3)

```
          SUMY=SUM(N,Y,Z)
C
CØMMENT--CØMPUTE REGRESSIØN CØEFFICIENTS
C
          DENØM=XN*SUMXX-SUMX**2
          AZERØ=(SUMY*SUMXX-SUMX*SUMXY)/DENØM
          AØNE=(XN*SUMXY-SUMX*SUMY)/DENØM
C
CØMMENT--WRITE ØUT DATA
C
          WRITE(6,1001)(X(J),Y(J),J=1,N)
     1001 FØRMAT('1INPUT DATA        X        Y'/(11X,2F10.2))
          WRITE (6,1002)AZERØ,AØNE
     1002 FØRMAT(///' THE EQUATIØN ØF THE BEST'
         1' STRAIGHT LINE IS  Y = ',F8.2,' + ',F8.2,' X')
C
CØMMENT--USE DØUBLE SUBSCRIPTED VARIABLE TØ
C          PREPARE GRAPH PLACE DØTS IN ARRAY TØ
C          REPRESENT AXES
C
          DØ 1003 J=1,100
          GRAPH(101,J)=DØT
          GRAPH(J,1)=DØT
          DØ 1003 K=2,101
     1003 GRAPH(J,K)=BLANK
          GRAPH(101,101)=DØT
CØMMENT--FIND LARGEST DATA VALUE FØR SCALING
C
          BIG=0.0
          DØ 1004 I=1,100
          XI=I
          Z(I)=AZERØ+AØNE*XI
          IF(Z(I).GT.BIG)BIG=Z(I)
     1004 CØNTINUE
          FACTØR=100./BIG
          DØ 1005 I=1,N
     1005 Y(I)=Y(I)*FACTØR
C
CØMMENT--PLACE DØTS IN ARRAY TØ REPRESENT
C          STRAIGHT LINE
C
          DØ 1006 J=1,100
          Z(J)=Z(J)*FACTØR
```

```
          JY=Z(J)+0.5
     1006 GRAPH(101-JY,J+1)=DØT
C
CØMMENT--PLACE STARS IN ARRAY TØ REPRESENT
C          ØRIGINAL DATA PØINTS
C
          DØ 1007 J=1,N
          JX=X(J)+0.5
          JY=Y(J)+0.5
     1007 GRAPH(101-JY,JX+1)=STAR
C
CØMMENT--WRITE ØUT GRAPH
C
          WRITE(6,1011)
          DØ 1008 J=1,101
     1008 WRITE(6,1009)(GRAPH(J,K),K=1,101)
     1009 FØRMAT(1X,101A1)
          WRITE(6,1010)
     1010 FØRMAT('+',101X,'X')
     1011 FØRMAT(///' Y')
          STØP
          END
          FUNCTIØN SUM(J,A,B)
          DIMENSIØN A(101),B(101)
          SUM=0.0
          DØ 100 K=1,J
          SUM=SUM+A(K)*B(K)
      100 CØNTINUE
          RETURN
          END
```

It will be noted that the program above works only for positive values of both x and y, and certain ranges of values of x and y are necessary in order to obtain a usable and meaningful graph. It will be left to the reader to modify the program to fit other situations. Fig. 8-6 displays the results of this program for the set of data indicated in the top portion of the figure.

8-6 CONCLUSION

Although this chapter was titled "Applications," it has not even begun to scratch the surface as far as presenting the possible engineering applications of computers. Virtually any engineering

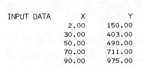

INPUT DATA   X   Y

              2.00   150.00
            30.00   403.00
            50.00   490.00
            70.00   711.00
            90.00   975.00

THE EQUATION OF THE BEST STRAIGHT LINE IS   Y =   109.11   +   9.02 X

Figure 8-6

problem that can be solved analytically can be programmed for computer solution. The purpose of this chapter has been to present a few different types of problems encountered in engineering applications. It is hoped that you (presumed to be a freshman engineering student) will begin to see the wide applicability and utility of the computer and will accordingly use it extensively in your future career as a student and subsequently as an engineer. The key to success is an initial enthusiasm to explore the enormous number of possible powerful techniques that you can now apply.

8-7 PROBLEMS

8-1 Write a program that will plot a graph of y as a function of x for the equation
$$y = 3.19x + 2.60 \quad \text{for } 1 < x < 30$$

8-2 Repeat Problem 8-1 for the equation
$$y = x^{0.7} + 20 \quad \text{for } 1 < x < 50$$

8-3 Repeat Problem 8-1 for the equation
$$y = -x^3 + 8x^2 + 5 \quad \text{for } 1 < x < 20$$
(Note that some values of y will be negative and also that a "scale factor" will be required. It might be helpful to have the computer write out a table of x and y values to determine a scale factor.)

8-4 Use the program of Example 8-1 to determine the depth of flow for the following:
$$Q = 3330 \text{ ft}^3/\text{sec}$$
$$W = 30 \text{ ft}$$
$$n = 0.013$$
$$S = 0.001$$

8-5 Use the program of Example 8-2 to determine the roots of the equation
$$1.06 \ x^4 + 8.12 \ x^3 - 24.90x^2 - 44.00x + 59.01 = 0$$

8-6 A simple electrical circuit, shown on Fig. 8-7, consists of two loops

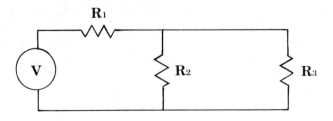

Figure 8-7

and a voltage source and three resistors. This system can be analyzed by the following matrix equation.

$$
\begin{vmatrix} (R_1+R_2) & (-R_3) \\ (-R_3) & (R_2+R_3) \end{vmatrix}
\begin{vmatrix} I_I \\ I_{II} \end{vmatrix}
=
\begin{vmatrix} V \\ 0 \end{vmatrix}
$$

If the values of the voltage (V) and the three resistors (R_1, R_2, and R_3) are known, the values of the mesh currents (I_I and I_{II}) can be determined by solving the matrix equation as follows:

$$
\begin{vmatrix} I_I \\ I_{II} \end{vmatrix}
=
\frac{\begin{vmatrix} (R_2+R_3) & (R_3) \\ (R_3) & (R_1+R_2) \end{vmatrix} \begin{vmatrix} V \\ 0 \end{vmatrix}}{(R_1+R_2)(R_2+R_3) - R_3^{\,2}}
$$

Write a program that will solve this problem.

8-7 Revise the program written for Example 8-4 so that it will handle values of x and y, each ranging from -100 to +100.

8-8 Revise Problem 6-20 to write a program that will determine the date on which either the highest temperature, the lowest temperature, or the maximum precipitation occurred between any two dates that are input to the program. Input should consist of the two dates and a code number that tells whether the highest temperature, the lowest temperature, or the maximum precipitation is desired. A subroutine would be useful for this program.

9
Advanced
Fortran IV Topics

The first eight chapters provide an introduction to individuals who desire to learn how to use Fortran for general applications. For beginning programmers, the coverage provided is actually all that is needed until the programs attempted become large enough that some programming "efficiency" is desired. The topics covered in this chapter are not really "advanced" from the standpoint of being more highly theoretical, but are "advanced" in that they could be used to separate "plug and chug" programs from programs that take advantage of the Fortran compiler's composition.

The coverage of these topics will be divided into two overall classes — type declaration statements (Sec. 9-1 through Sec. 9-5) and assorted concepts useful with subprograms (Sec. 9-6 through Sec. 9-9). Some of these topics may vary in exact usage from compiler to compiler; thus the reader is urged to check the reference manual for the Fortran compiler being used for specific requirements prior to employing topics in this chapter in a program.

9-1 REAL AND INTEGER STATEMENTS

In Chap. 2, the naming of variables was shown to be based on the first-letter rule; i.e., integer variable names begin with the letters I through N and real variable names begin with the letters A through H and Ø through Z. Up to this point, this naming implication has been followed. But, what about situations in which a programmer desires to associate a real constant with a variable name that begins with one of the letters I - N?

For example, the variable MØNEY could possibly be assigned the value 138.35 representing $138.35. One may assign the integer name MØNEY and just let the compiler truncate the value to 138. To prevent this one could rename the variable XMØNEY. Another way to circumvent the problem — which leaves the name MØNEY unchanged — is to use the REAL statement. This type-statement is of the form:

REAL a,b,c

where a, b, c may be the names of variables, arrays, or functions. This (and any) type-statement is used to override or confirm the implicit typing of a name. For example, in the following example

REAL MØNEY

the variable MØNEY is now a real variable and may retain the value 138.35. The REAL statement may also be used to establish the size of an array as in a DIMENSIØN statement. If MØNEY is to be a real array of 15 values, the following could be used:

REAL MØNEY(15)

No DIMENSIØN statement would be necessary if this REAL statement was included in a program.

In a similar situation, a programmer may wish to use a variable name to store only integer values, and the name may not begin with the letters I through N. For example, suppose the names CASES or FLIGHT may have only integer values. CASES could be renamed ICASES, but FLIGHT would have to be renamed IFLIGH or something else. Why? Obviously a little is lost to the programmer in the connotation of each of the renamed variables. The original names can be maintained — and integer values assumed — by the use of the INTEGER type-statement. Consider:

INTEGER CASES, FLIGHT

This will insure that the variables CASES and FLIGHT will be integer variables for the entire program unit.

The names of function subprograms may also be declared to be real or integer variable names as in the following FUNCTIØN statements:

REAL FUNCTIØN JAM(A,B)
          or
INTEGER FUNCTIØN SUM(X,Y)

9-2 THE IMPLICIT STATEMENT

Another method of typing variables is to use the IMPLICIT statement. This statement redefines the first-letter rule. For example, if we wish to reverse the first-letter rule (i.e., to have integer variable names begin with the letters A through H and Ø through Z and real variable names begin with the letters I through N), the following statement should appear as the first statement in a program:

IMPLICIT INTEGER(A-H,Ø-Z),REAL(I-N)

With this statement, CASES and FLIGHT would be integer variables, and MØNEY would be a real variable. An alternative for the CASES/FLIGHT/MØNEY example would be:

IMPLICIT INTEGER(C,F),REAL(M)

Note that single letters or ranges of letters may be used in the IMPLICIT statement. More than one IMPLICIT statement may appear in a program unit; however, the same letter — whether by itself or included in a range — may only appear once in all the IMPLICIT statements of that program unit. Subsequent type-statements may override the IMPLICIT typing. For example in the following

IMPLICIT INTEGER(G-N)
REAL HØUSE

all variable names starting with the letter H except HØUSE will be integers.

9-3 THE DØUBLE PRECISIØN STATEMENT

In scientific and engineering experiments, measurements may at times be made with great accuracy. Application of the data obtained may require numerous calculations. Because of the limitations for storing values assigned to the standard real or integer variables, a roundoff error may occur with each expression. In order to avoid the "snowball" effect in rounding, as more computations are encountered, an extension of the normal storage space will allow more digits to be retained from evaluations. Thus less roundoff error will occur.

Most computers will allow approximately twice the normal space for values to be stored if desired. Depending on the computer, this would mean a single number could have 8 to 18 digits that would be maintained in memory. Constants must be entered using a "D" exponent form. This denotes the constant as being double precision. For example

123.4567898D 04

is a double precision constant equal to 123.4567898×10^4. Double precision variables must be distinguished from standard precision variables by the DØUBLE PRECISION statement — another type-statement.

DØUBLE PRECISIØN A,J(10)

In this statement the variable A and all ten elements of array J will be of double precision type. (The DØUBLE PRECISIØN statement serves in this instance to "dimension" the variable J, and no DIMENSIØN statement is required.) Assignment statements may be used to assign values as usual. Consider:

A=45.3720165D0

The value assigned to double precision variable A is a double precision constant. Double precision values may also be transferred into and transmitted from a program using input/output statements. The format entry designation Dw.d is used. This designation is identical to Ew.d as explained in Chap. 3, except that D is used to separate the decimal number from the appropriate exponent of ten.

Other than the difference in establishing a double precision variable and assigning its value, computations and usage of values are the same as for standard precision values. One warning is necessary. Be sure *all* variables that are to be assigned double precision values are declared to be of the double precision type. For example consider this illustration.

DØUBLE PRECISIØN F,G,H
F=7.18D5
G=98.7654321D0
H=F*G

If H had not been inclued in the DØUBLE PRECISIØN statement, the value assigned to H would not have been double precision.

Statement function names and the names of function subprograms may also be made double precision. The following skeleton program will exemplify both:

DØUBLE PRECISIØN QUANT,C,D,VALUE
QUANT(A,B)=(A*B)/2.3
X=9.52217
Y=100.0058
C=QUANT(X,Y)
.
.

.
D=VALUE(C)

.

.

.

STØP
END
DØUBLE PRECISIØN FUNCTIØN VALUE(H)
DØUBLE PRECISIØN H

.

.

.

RETURN
END

Note that not only should the name of the statement function (QUANT) or function subprogram (VALUE) appear in the DØUBLE PRECISIØN statement, but also the variables to which assignments are made (C, D, and H). Many of the built-in functions will accept double precision arguments.

9-4 THE CØMPLEX STATEMENT

In many engineering problems another situation that a programmer may encounter is handling complex numbers (for example, 4 + 6i). In Fortran, the complex number is represented by a pair of real or integer constants separated by a comma, and the pair is grouped in parentheses. The constant on the left represents the "real" part of the complex number, whereas the constant on the right represents the "imaginary" part. The illustrations below demonstrate the representation of complex numbers in Fortran.

Mathematical Quantity	Fortran Representation As A Complex Constant
2.3 + 0.4i	(2.3,0.4)
1.0	(1.0,0.0)
-15.i	(0.0,-15.)

Complex variables must be declared in a type-statement. The general form is:

CØMPLEX a,b,c

where a, b, c represents a list of names of variables, arrays, and/or functions separated by commas. The names follow the usual rules for naming variables (Chap.2) except that the first letter is unimportant (no integer or real complex numbers). If an array is to contain complex values, its dimensions may be defined in a CØMPLEX statement, as:

CØMPLEX C(10),INT

The array C will be complex and contain 10 subscripted complex variables. INT will be a single complex variable. Note that there is no need for a DIMENSIØN statement to declare the size of the array C.

Given the CØMPLEX statement example, C(5) and INT could be assigned values as follows in a program:

C(5)=(4.23,5.1)
INT=(0.01,4.23)

To use input/output statements with complex variables in the read/write lists requires that the programmer provide two format entry designations for each value to be transferred. Consider:

```
      CØMPLEX CMPLX
      CMPLX=(1.4,2.2)
      WRITE(6,100)CMPLX
100   FØRMAT(1X,2F5.1)
      STØP
      END
```

This program, if compiled and executed, would produce:

Printed Position	1	2	3	4	5	6	7	8	9	10
Data			1	.	4			2	.	2

Arithmetic operations performed using complex variables would conform to manipulation of complex numbers as shown in:

```
      CØMPLEX A23,B31,C43
      A23=(1.2,3.6)
      B31=(6.5,8.2)
      C43=A23+B31
      WRITE(6,105)C43
100   FØRMAT(1X,'C43=',2F5.1)
      STØP
      END
```

The output would be:

Printed Position	1	2	3	4	5	6	7	8	9	10	11	12	13	14
Data	C	4	3	=			7	.	7		1	1	.	8

Again, the programmer must insure that all variables or functions that are to receive complex constants as values be declared in a CØMPLEX statement. As with DØUBLE PRECISIØN, there exist a few built-in functions to deal with complex arithmetic — obtaining the complex conjugate, separation of real and imaginary quantities, and conversion of real numbers to complex numbers, to name a few.

9-5 THE LØGICAL STATEMENT

In Chap. 5, the logical IF statement was introduced. In this section other forms of logical values are presented. Just as there may be real constants, integer constants, and complex constants, there may also exist logical constants. In the logical IF statement the expression in parentheses was shown to have a value of true or false. For example:

IF(X.GT.100.)GØ TØ 250
GØ TØ 150

In the above IF statement the value of the expression in parentheses (true or false) indicates whether control will be transferred to statement 150 or statement 250. If the expression is true (X>100.), then control goes to statement 250; if false (X≤100.), control goes to statement 150.

There are only two logical constants in Fortran — .TRUE. and .FALSE.. Note the inclusion of the decimals. Logical constants are of importance in determining the value of logical expressions as seen in the logical IF statement. One may also want to assign values to logical variables.

Many problems encountered in scientific and engineering work involve situations in which two outcomes, results, or decisions are possible. Simple electrical circuits are modelled, for example, using 'either or' logic — either current is present or it is not. Trying to deal with problems of this nature using numerical quantities is possible but not as convenient or practical as using logical values. If current is present a variable representing the circuit could have a value of .TRUE.; if absent the variable would have a value of .FALSE.. When circuits are combined, a network of logical variables could be established and results related to the entire circuit.

The method of declaring variables to be of logical type is through the LØGICAL statement. This statement is of the form:

LØGICAL a,b,c

where a, b, c are the names of variables, arrays, or functions
separated by commas. The naming of logical variables is the same
as for other variables. As with other type-statements, array size
may be declared in the LØGICAL statement as:

LØGICAL X(10)

This establishes a logical array X with 10 elements, each capable of
having only .TRUE. or .FALSE. for a value. The value of each
element of array X could be set to .TRUE. by the following
statements:

LØGICAL X(10)
DØ 100 I=1,10
X(I)=.TRUE.
100 CØNTINUE

The third statement above is a logical assignment statement. To
the right of the "=" must be a logical expression. When the logical
expression is evaluated, the result is assigned as the value of the
logical variable on the left of the "=". For example, the following
could appear in a later statement, continuing the above example:

X(2)=X(1).AND.A.GT.B*3.2

where A and B are two real variables and .AND. is a logical
operator. Obviously a hierarchy or precedence of operators must be
given for operators used in logical expressions like the one
involving real variables and constants.

The complete hierarchy of operators is as follows:

Parenthetical expressions
function references
**
* and /
+ and -
relational operators .EQ.,.NE.,.GE.
.GT.,.LE.,.LT.
.NOT. ⎫
.AND. ⎬ **logical operators**
.OR. ⎭

The arithmetic operators and relational operators were defined in

Chap. 5. Each of the relational operators is of the same hierarchical level. Thus if more than one relational operator is found in a logical expression, the left-most operator is used with its operands first; then the operator to its right is used; and so on. The lowest levels of operators are the logical operators — .NØT., .AND., and .ØR.. The operator .NØT. takes precedence over .AND., which takes precedence over .ØR..

Using these ideas, let's evaluate the preceding statement:

X(2)=X(1).AND.A.GT.B*3.2

If X(1) has a value of .TRUE., A a value of 2.0, and B a value of 1.0, we can now evaluate this logical expression. Three operators are included in the expression: .AND., .GT., and *. The order of usage of the operators will be *, .GT., and .AND.. B*3.2 will produce a value of 3.2. The value of A (2.0) will then be compared to the product 3.2 using the operator .GT.. Since 2.0 is *not* greater than 3.2, the result of this comparison is .FALSE.. Finally the value of X(1) (.TRUE.) will be compared with .FALSE. using the logical operator .AND.. Since both operands are not .TRUE., the result of the evaluation will be .FALSE.. Thus the value assigned to the logical variable X(2) will be .FALSE..

Evaluations using the three logical operators may be best demonstrated using the table below:

Value of logical operand No. 1	logical operator	Value of logical operand No. 2	Result of Evaluation
.TRUE.	.AND.	.TRUE.	.TRUE.
.TRUE.	.AND.	.FALSE.	.FALSE.
.FALSE.	.AND.	.TRUE.	.FALSE.
.FALSE.	.AND.	.FALSE.	.FALSE.
.TRUE.	.ØR.	.TRUE.	.TRUE.
.TRUE.	.ØR.	.FALSE.	.TRUE.
.FALSE.	.ØR.	.TRUE.	.TRUE.
.FALSE.	.ØR.	.FALSE.	.FALSE.
No preceding operand	.NØT.	.TRUE.	.FALSE.
	.NØT.	.FALSE.	.TRUE.

Values of logical variables may also be assigned through input/output statements. The FØRMAT entry designation used with logical variables is Lw. The w represents the width of the field in which the value is to appear. On input, some compilers allow no decimals to appear in the value. Actually, a T or an F is all that is needed. Thus a format of L1 on input should suffice for practically every situation in which logical constant input is needed. On output, the letters T and F are printed with "w-1" leading blanks. For example consider:

```
    LØGICAL ABE
    ABE=.TRUE.
    WRITE(6,200)ABE
200 FØRMAT(1X,L5)
    STØP
    END
```

Upon execution of the above, the following would be produced:

Printed Position 1 2 3 4 5 6 7
Data   T

Note four blanks precede the "T".

The names of statement functions and function subprograms may be of logical type. However, again it is necessary that the programmer declare all variables that are to be assigned logical constants within a LØGICAL statement.

NOTE: Before leaving type-declaration statements, one fact must be emphasized. A variable name must appear only once in any *type* statement in a program unit. For example, the following would be erroneous:

```
REAL MAN
LØGICAL MAN
  .
  .
  .
END
```

9-6 THE CØMMØN STATEMENT

As implied in Chap. 7, there exist other means of having data available to various program units than through the association of actual arguments with dummy arguments. Just as data are available for usage within a single program unit (by referring to a variable name), the CØMMØN statement allows access by two or more program units to data stored in memory.

The CØMMØN statement is of the form:

CØMMØN a,b,c

where a, b, c are the names of variables or arrays. The dimensions of an array may be defined in the CØMMØN statement. No function names are allowed in the CØMMØN statement. Consider this statement in a main program:

CØMMØN X,Y

This CØMMØN statement declares that the values of X and Y for the program unit in which this statement appears will occupy the first two locations of the "blank" common area of memory. If in a subprogram (of a complete Fortran program), the following appeared:

CØMMØN R,S

then the values R and S would actually be the same as X and Y, respectively, from the main program. This is similar to the situation in which R and S are dummy arguments in the subprogram, and X and Y are actual arguments in a main program reference to the subprogram. Actually, however, R and S changed every time X and Y change; and vice-versa. (Note: the programmer should insure that variables sharing the same memory locations are of the same type, i.e., X and R are both *real* variables.)

The memory locations are position oriented in the CØMMØN statement. All first position names in CØMMØN statements refer to the same memory locations; all second position names refer to the same memory locations, etc. Consider the following:

Mainprogram .

.

CØMMØN X,Y,Z
X=5.
Y=6.
15 Z=7.

.

.

.

.

END

.

.

.

Subprogram No. 1   .

       .

CØMMØN A,B

       .

       .

       .

       .

END

Subprogram No. 2   .

       .

CØMMØN R,S,T

       .

       .

       .

       .

END

When statement 15 is executed in the main program, A will have a value of 5. in subprogram No. 1 and R will also have a value of 5. in subprogram No. 2; B will have a value of 6. in subprogram No. 1 and S will also have a value of 6. in subprogram No. 2; finally, T will have a value of 7. in subprogram No. 2. (Values for all five of these variables may change prior to their usage in the subprograms.)

Areas of CØMMØN may be "labelled" so as to help the programmer with position orientation responsibilities in using CØMMØN. Slashes must precede and follow a CØMMØN area name. The names of the variables in that area will follow the second slash. An example of a labelled CØMMØN usage is:

Mainprogram: .

       .

       .

CØMMØN /BLK1/A,B,C/BLK2/
A=3.2
B=4.5
C=7.8
X=1.0
25 Y=2.0

       .

       .

       .

	END
Subprogram No. 1:	.
	.
	.
	CØMMØN /BLK1/R,S,T
	.
	.
	.
	END
Subprogram No. 2:	.
	.
	.
	CØMMØN /BLK2/G,H
	.
	.
	.
	END

When statement 25 is executed in the main program, R, S, and T will have values 3.2, 4.5, and 7.8, respectively, in subprogram No. 1. Variables G and H in subprogram No. 2 will have values 1.0 and 2.0, respectively. Notice that G and H, which are associated with X and Y in the main program, can be referred to in subprogram No. 2 without having to include BLK1 in the CØMMØN statement of subprogram No. 2. Thus labelling common areas helps the programmer with position orientation of variables in CØMMØN.

9-7 THE EQUIVALENCE STATEMENT

Often a programmer will construct a long program from smaller programs that may be debugged and tested at different times and/or for different purposes. After combining the parts, it may occur that one entity in one part represented the same entity in another part. Because of the freedom of naming variables, the two entities may have different variable names. One recourse for the programmer is to make changes in the program statements so as to produce an agreement for all variable names that represent the same entity. For example, the sum of five values may be represented by the variable SUM in one program part. Likewise the sum may be represented by the variable TØTAL in another part. The process of changing the program statements could be time-

consuming. One way to avoid this is through use of the EQUIVA-
LENCE statement. This statement is of the general form:

EQUIVALENCE (a,b),(c,d)

where a, b, c, d are variable names, arrays, or elements of arrays.
Function names are not allowed in the EQUIVALENCE statement.
The SUM/TØTAL example above would be solved using:

EQUIVALENCE (SUM,TØTAL)

The EQUIVALENCE statement is used to show which variables,
arrays, or elements of an array will share the same memory location. SUM and TØTAL would always refer to the same location,
thus, they would always identify the same summation of the five
values. (Note: as with the CØMMØN statement, the programmer
must insure that the variables sharing the same memory locations
are of the same data type; i.e., SUM and TØTAL above are both real
variables.)

In the SUM/TØTAL example, a savings of space is realized also
since only *one* memory location is now reserved for the summation.
A more significant storage savings may be realized if two or more
variables or arrays are used separately in two different parts of a
program. Consider

DIMENSIØN G(50,150),H(50,150)
EQUIVALENCE (G,H)

By assigning the same locations for the 7500 locations of storage to
the G and H arrays, the effort saves 7500 storage locations of
memory. Again, the calculations to be performed involving G
should be completely separate from those involving H to insure no
data mixup. In this example also note locations for G(1,1) and
H(1,1) will match; likewise, for G(2,1) and H(2,1) ... and G(50,150)
and H(50,150). This is provided for when the array *names* G and H
are used in the EQUIVALENCE statements.

The order of matching will be determined as above for arrays G
and H or a different order as specifically directed by the programmer using the notation of the beginning element for one or all
arrays. The following example will demonstrate:

DIMENSIØN C(5),D(5)
EQUIVALENCE (C(3),D(2))

In this example, C(3) is first matched with D(2), then C(4) with D(3), then C(5) with D(4); no more elements in C can be matched with D(5) — thus this element does not share its memory location with any other variable. The element C(2) would also be matched with D(1), and C(1) could not be matched with any variable, so C(1) does not share its memory location with any other variable.

To combine the last two examples, if no subscript is given for an array in an EQUIVALENCE statement, the matching of variables begins with the first storage locations of both arrays (first element of first column). This process of matchings continues for all elements of both arrays. If subscripts are specified, then the matchings begin with the element named. As shown in the C/D example above, some elements may not share memory locations, e.g. C(1) and D(5).

One other use of the EQUIVALENCE statement is to use variables to reference particular values in a program. For example, consider:

    CØMPLEX E
    DIMENSIØN F(2)
    EQUIVALENCE (F,E)

Thus F(1) would share the same memory location as the real value of complex variable F, and F(2) would share the same memory location as the imaginary part of complex variable E. The real and imaginary parts of E can be referenced easily and individually by using elements of array F.

9-8 THE ENTRY STATEMENT

Frequently the computations performed in a subprogram involve two or more sets of computations. For example, a function subprogram which is used to compute the mean and standard deviation of a set of values will include four basic computations — summing the values, computing the mean, summing squared differences, and computing the square root. Below is a subprogram to find the mean and standard deviation of a set of data.

```
        SUBRØUTINE MEANSD(A,N,XMEAN,STDEV)
C
C       SUBPRØGRAM TØ CALCULATE A MEAN AND
C       STANDARD DEVIATION
C
        DIMENSIØN A(100)
```

```
C
C          SUM VALUES
C
           SUM=0.0
           XN=N
           DØ 10 I=1,N
           SUM=SUM+A(I)
        10 CØNTINUE
C
C          CØMPUTE MEAN
C
           XMEAN=SUM/XN
C
C          SUM SQUARED DIFFERENCES
C
           SUM=0.0
           DØ 20 I=1,N
           SUM=SUM+(A(I)-XMEAN)**2
        20 CØNTINUE
C
C          FIND SQUARE RØØT ØF SUM ØF SQUARED
C          DIFFERENCES DIVIDED BY N
C
           STDEV=SQRT(SUM/XN)
           RETURN
           END
```

Having the standard deviation for a set of raw data may be desirable at one point in a program. But suppose the mean had already been determined prior to one execution of this same program. Would the programmer have to construct a completely separate program to sum the squared differences and then find the standard deviation? The answer is no. The ENTRY statement will allow the programmer to utilize only the last portion of the original subprogram in order to compute the standard deviation.

The ENTRY statement is of the form:

ENTRY name(a,b,c)

where name is any name for the subprogram subset chosen according to the same considerations for the subprogram name. The dummy arguments a, b, and c represent a list of possible arguments. These arguments do not have to correspond to the FUNCTIØN statement or SUBRØUTINE statement arguments;

nor must a, b, c agree with any other ENTRY statement arguments. Of course, a, b, c must agree in order, number, and type with the actual arguments in the reference to the entry point.

The reference to an entry point consists of the use of the "name" in an expression in some program unit if the ENTRY statement is in a function subprogram; otherwise the reference is made via a "CALL name" statement in a program unit. Reference to an ENTRY statement may be made by any program unit, except the one in which the ENTRY statement appears.

Let's examine the changes necessary in the preceding subprogram that will provide an alternate entry point.

```
          SUBRØUTINE MEANSD(A,N,XMEAN,STDEV)
C
C         SUBPRØGRAM TØ CALCULATE A MEAN AND
C         STANDARD DEVIATIØN
C
          DIMENSIØN A(100)
C
C         SUM VALUES
C
          SUM=0.0
          XN=N
          DØ 10 I=1,N
          SUM=SUM+A(I)
       10 CØNTINUE
C
C         CØMPUTE MEAN
C
          XMEAN=SUM/XN
C
C         SUM SQUARED DIFFERENCES
C
          ENTRY SD(A,N,XMEAN,STDEV)
          SUM=0.0
          XN=N
          DØ 20 I=1,N
          SUM=SUM+(A(I)-XMEAN)**2
       20 CØNTINUE
C
C         FIND SQUARE RØØT ØF SUM ØF SQUARED
C         DIFFERENCES DIVIDED BY N
C
```

```
STDEV=SQRT(SUM/XN)
RETURN
END
```

Note that the only difference is the inclusion of the ENTRY SD statement in subroutine MEANSD. Statement ENTRY SD is a non-executable statement and will cause no change in execution if the normal entry is made to subroutine MEANSD. The subroutine now can be used to calculate the mean and standard deviation of a set of up to 100 values or can be used to calculate only the standard deviation of the set of values if the mean of the set is known. Since two separate subprograms did not have to be constructed, memory space is saved. Additionally, any subprogram may have as many entry points as needed. Finally, references to all and part of subroutine MEANSD are given below:

```
Main program    DIMENSIØN X(100),Y(100)
                READ(5,10)M,(X(I),I=1,M)
                  .
                  .
                  .
                CALL MEANSD(X,M,XM,XSD)
                  .
                  .
                  .
                READ(5,100)I,(Y(J),J=1,I),XM2
                  .
                  .
                  .
                CALL SD(Y,I,XM2,XSD)
                  .
                  .
                  .
                STØP
                END
```

The first CALL statement references the entire subroutine MEANSD. The second CALL statement references the subset of subroutine MEANSD beginning after the ENTRY SD statement. XSD is the only output received from the reference to ENTRY SD.

9-9 ADJUSTABLE ARRAYS

Some compilers allow a programmer to specify the size of arrays used in subprograms at the time the subprogram is executed. In so doing, the programmer does not have to change a subprogram each time the size of the arrays must be changed; nor does the subprogram unnecessarily use up extra storage space.

There are four restrictions on the use of adjustable arrays:

1) A main program may never contain an adjustable array; only subprograms;
2) At least one dummy argument list of the subprogram must contain the name of the adjustable array;
3) The size of the adjustable array must be specified by an integer variable which is a dummy argument of the subprogram;
4) The value of the dummy argument specifying the size of the adjustable array may not exceed the size of the actual array in the calling program.

These are demonstrated below:

Main Program

```
          DIMENSIØN X(100)
          READ(5,10)I,(X(J),J=1,I)
       10 FØRMAT(I5,(10F4.0))
          SUM=TØTAL(X,I)
          WRITE(6,50)SUM
       50 FØRMAT('1SUM = ',F10.5)
          STØP
          END
```

Function TØTAL

```
          FUNCTIØN TØTAL(A,N)
  C
  C       SUBPRØGRAM TØ SUM N VALUES ØF
  C       THE A ARRAY
  C
          DIMENSIØN A(N)
          TØTAL=0.0
          DØ 10 I=1,N
```

```
        TØTAL=TØTAL+A(I)
   10 CØNTINUE
        RETURN
        END
```

Notice that the size of the array X in the main program is defined by the integer *constant* 100, whereas in the function TØTAL the size of the array A is defined by the integer *variable* N. Both A and N are dummy arguments in function TØTAL. The value of I supplied as an actual argument in the main program must not exceed 100.

9-10 A COMMENT

Before concluding the chapter, the authors wish to point out that the topics included in this chapter are by no means the *only* advanced topics. Indeed, some of these topics are simply techniques of efficiency in programming. For short, simple programs the savings realized by employment of any of the techniques described may seem meaningless. Additionally, other techniques, deemed less applicable by the majority of programmers, have been omitted. This was partly due to the desire to omit unnecessary topics from this beginner's text, partly because the usages of many of these techniques are highly variable from one computer system to another, and partly from the authors' own experiences.

9-11 PROBLEMS

In Problems 9-1 through 9-8 state what is wrong, if anything, with the statement(s) given.

9-1   FUNCTIØN REAL MAN(X,Y,Ƶ)

9-2   DBLE PRECISIØN MINUTE

9-3   IMPLICIT REAL(A-H,I,K)

9-4   CØMMØN BLK/A,B,C/

9-5   EQUALENCE (IAVG,MEAN)

9-6   SUBRØUTINE SUM(A,I)
       DIMENSIØN A(J)

9-7   CALL ENTRY AVG

9-8   CØMPLEX CØNJ
       CØNJ=(1,0,2.0i)

9-9 Give the coding required to have the *letters* A through F and T through X be first letters for all real variable names and all other letters be first letters for integer variable names.

9-10 Give the coding (if any) necessary to render the variable names — DØG, CØAT, NIGHT:
   a) Double precision
   b) Integer
   c) Real
   d) Logical

9-11 In computing the probability of occurrence of different readings taken from an experiment over a period of time, one can normalize the distribution of values. This involves simply summing the values of the readings and dividing the sum by the number of readings taken. Assume you have taken 50 readings, and you wish to find the probability of each reading occurring. Construct a program that "reads in" the values in the main program and calls a function subprogram to compute the normalized distribution. Have a common area to transfer values to and from the subprogram.

9-12 Reconstruct the program for Problem 9-11. In this case have the values (up to 100 readings possible) "read in" in the main program, transferred to a function subprogram as actual arguments in the function reference. The function should then compute and print out the normalized distribution.

10
Closure

Having covered the topics necessary to develop useful Fortran programs, a few assorted ideas related to the usage of Fortran and programming itself need to be addressed. This chapter will briefly recap the characteristics of Fortran and the results achieved in this programming manual. Following this we will offer some ideas on both the implementation and other possible uses of Fortran — separate from those suggested in the previous chapters. Finally, the future utilization of programming in general will be examined.

10-1 FORTRAN RECAP/RESULTS ACHIEVED

Taking an overview of the material presented in this book, it may be stated that all Fortran programs are composed of input segments, data manipulation segments, and output segments. The techniques of structuring these segments in Fortran were addressed in Chap. 2 through Chap. 9. Obviously, the input segments are crucially important in obtaining correct results from any computations. Likewise, correct answers from computations are useless if the output segment is not correctly formulated to transmit the answers. The authors will not attempt to review all of the Fortran commands introduced, but will here emphasize again the importance of correct formulation and integration of general segments in a Fortran program.

The applications covered in this book should suggest that Fortran can be used in a broad range of problems. Actually the creativity of the user is the limiting factor in the application of Fortran. For this reason, the authors have tried to expose the beginning programmer (the reader) to many different problems in a variety of disciplines in science and engineering. Simultaneously, flowcharts have been presented to emphasize the generic parts of each program, as well as the logical sequence of introduction of these parts. Ideas presented in the example problems and exercises should provide a "spawning ground" for the reader in applying Fortran to any desired area.

10-2 IMPLEMENTATION

The actual process of implementing a Fortran program just begins with an error-free "run" of a program. Once the program produces answers, the programmer must then seek to validate his or her program and results. Often a check of results achieved with available data from the situation modelled will indicate either errors in the logic (as structured in the flowchart) or errors in the set of Fortran statements which supposedly reflected the operations indicated in the flowchart. Each programmer is the best judge of which situation exists, but subtleties of a particular problem may require outside help in correcting the faulty results. For example, an equation may be applicable only over a certain range of the value of a variable; outside of this range, it may be invalid and another equation may apply. Consider the following situation involving the approximation of $\tan^{-1}X$:*

$$\tan^{-1} x = x - \frac{x^3}{3} + \frac{x^5}{5} - \frac{x^7}{7} + \cdots \qquad \text{if } (-1 < x > 1)$$

$$\tan^{-1} x = \frac{\pi}{2} - \frac{1}{x} + \frac{1}{3x^3} - \frac{1}{5x^5} + \frac{1}{7x^7} - \cdots \qquad \text{if } (x > 1)$$

$$\tan^{-1} x = -\frac{\pi}{2} - \frac{1}{x} + \frac{1}{3x^3} - \frac{1}{5x^5} + \frac{1}{7x^7} - \cdots \qquad \text{if } (x < -1)$$

A programmer not realizing the difference in the series necessary to approximate $\tan^{-1}X$ for the appropriate interval in which X occurred may obtain an erroneous answer by correctly solving the wrong equation. The programmer in this situation would be probably certain that his or her program for summing the terms of the series was correct. Obviously the programmer should attempt to examine the entire problem formulation for possible errors rather than dwelling on the programming aspects in this situation. Again, sometimes outside assistance or input may help to spot the error with less frustration for the programmer.

---

*($\tan^{-1}X$ if X=1 is the case in which the angle is approximately 0.785 radians or 45°)

10-3 ADDITIONAL USES OF FORTRAN

As stated in the preface of this book, the authors observed a need for a beginning text in Fortran that could be used in a science or engineering curriculum. Notwithstanding, Fortran is universal in that problems in other curricula can be solved using Fortran. In social sciences, for example, analyses may be conducted on random surveys undertaken to determine the factors contributing to the existence of certain phenomena. Fortran could be employed by an investigator to help make deductions from survey data. Usually, however, the investigator may simply rely on prepared analysis "packages," which already include the Fortran coding (or coding in another computer language) to perform the desired analyses.

Likewise, in a business environment, one may wish, for example, to maintain a record of transactions involving a car loan amortization. Fortran again *could* be utilized to provide an amortization schedule, but other programming languages (CØBØL for example) may be used. A major advantage of learning Fortran is that for virtually any problem, Fortran may be applied. Fortran can solve social science problems, business problems, perform mathematical manipulations, and solve engineering and science problems.

Not all problems in engineering and science have to be solved by custom-made programs, however, because programming "packages" have been developed to perform many frequently encountered operations — such as inverting a matrix or computing the area of a parcel of land. However, students of engineering and science will likely encounter many other problems that do need to be solved using custom-made programs. At the same time a programmer should be aware of pre-programmed algorithms that are available in any area of possible programming interest. Often persons working in computer centers can give information on sources of algorithms.

10-4 THE FUTURE UTILIZATION OF PROGRAMMING

Programming is obviously beneficial to users, particularly when applying special purpose algorithms. When algorithms gain acceptance among problem-solvers, then the availability of preprogrammed software increases. Thus, problem-solvers may opt to use the prepared algorithms rather than undertake the formulation of an original program themselves. As long as algorithms need to be developed for special-purpose situations, then programming will remain as a desired skill for a problem-solver or at least for someone designated to help the program-solver. This is true in all fields of endeavor. The following paragraphs illustrate some examples of situations occurring everyday, in which useful programming must be performed.

In engineering, for example, a problem-solver may be trying to determine the reliability of an electronic component that has been designed. If the design is unique, then the programming of the reliability calculations would best be performed by an individual knowledgeable in the component's design.

Personnel involved in the operations section of a bank are responsible for structuring the flow of information into the bank's automated general ledger. This would require programming that is customized for this bank.

Political scientists often need to thoroughly analyze the results of polls of citizens. Their analyses are usually performed with the aid of computer programs developed to generate statistical evidence from the poll data. These programs, and others developed to help analyze and prepare conclusions, are often custom-made.

From these brief examples, one may conclude that programming on an individual basis is here to stay. Actually, easy-to-understand computer software has recently been developed which make the utilization of computers by programming attractive to people in virtually any field in which manipulation of numbers is of value.

10-5 ONE LAST OPINION

The topics covered in Chap. 1 through Chap. 9 have, it is hoped, provided the starting point for problem-solving in Fortran on *any* computer having a Fortran compiler. Careful use of the Fortran concepts as presented herein, coupled with unyielding "debugging" persistence in your "computer center", will change a beginning programmer into a wise (maybe weary) veteran programmer. In developing each set of ideas, the authors have tried to forewarn the reader of common pitfalls; take heed of these, but do not be discouraged if you do not succeed initially. Learn from mistakes — experience is the *best* teacher!

Appendices

APPENDIX A
Fortran Built-in Functions

The following table presents useful function subprograms that are available with many Fortran processors. This list constitutes a portion of the "Intrinsic Functions" that are defined in American National Standard Fortran (ANSI X3.9-1978). The Fortran functions available on a particular computer (either as built-in or intrinsic functions) may vary as to number, exact name, or usage specifics. This appendix lists the most-often used and hopefully the most-frequently available functions. The Fortran reference manual for a particular computer should be consulted if the user encounters difficulty with the usage of the functions that follow.

The table provides four pieces of information for each function. The "Mathematical Definition" gives a brief indication of what the function subprogram accomplishes. The "Fortran Name Used" indicates the specific name which should be used in Fortran coding to reference the function desired. The type of the argument constant or expression used with the function name is given in the column "Argument Type (Input)". Some arguments must be real values, some integers, others double-precision or complex. The result of the function subprogram execution also has its own type as shown in the column "Function Type (Output)".

The types of data for both arguments and results will be represented by the following letters in the appendix:

    R = real
    I = integer
    D = double-precision
    C = complex

(Note: In using functions in this table with two arguments, both arguments must be of the same data type, i.e., both real or both double-precision, etc.)

Mathematical Definition	Fortran Name Used	Argument Type (Input)	Function Type (Output)
Square Root $\overline{\sqrt{\text{argument}}}$	SQRT DSQRT CSQRT	R D C	R D C
Absolute Value |argument|	ABS IABS DABS	R I D	R I D
Exponential e(argument)	EXP DEXP CEXP	R D C	R D C
Natural Logarithm ln (argument)	ALØG DLØG CLØG	R D C	R D C
Common Logarithm $\log_{10}$(argument)	ALØG10 DLØG10	R D	R D
Sine sin(argument)	SIN DSIN CSIN	R * D * C *	R D C
Cosine cos(argument)	CØS DCØS CCØS	R * D * C *	R D C
Tangent tan(argument)	TAN DTAN	R * D *	R D
Arcsine $\sin^{-1}$(argument)	ASIN DASIN	R D	R * D *
Arccosine $\cos^{-1}$(argument)	ACØS DACØS	R D	R * D *

* The angle involved will be in radians.

Mathematical Definition	Fortran Name Used	Argument Type (Input)	Function Type (Output)
Arctangent $\tan^{-1}(\text{argument})$ also - -	ATAN DATAN	R D	R * D *
$\tan^{-1}(\text{argument \#1/argument \#2})$	ATAN2 DATAN2	R D	R * D *
Hyperbolic Sine $\sinh(\text{argument})$	SINH DSINH	R * D *	R D
Hyperbolic Cosine $\cosh(\text{argument})$	CØSH DCØSH	R * D *	R D
Hyperbolic Tangent $\tanh(\text{argument})$	TANH DTANH	R * D *	R D
Selecting the largest value of a group $\max(\text{argument \#1,argument \#2,...})$ at least two arguments are required	MAX0 AMAX1 DMAX1 AMAX0 MAX1	I R D I R	I R D R I
Selecting the smallest value of a group $\min(\text{argument \#1,argument \#2,...})$ at least two arguments are required	MIṄ0 AMIN1 DMIN1 AMIN0 MIN1	I R D I R	I R D R I
Imaginary half of complex value b from a + bi	AIMAG	C	R

* The angle involved will be in radians.

Mathematical Definition	Fortran Name Used	Argument Type (Input)	Function Type (Output)
Real half of complex value a from a + bi	REAL	C	R
Conjugate of complex value a – (bi) from a + (bi) use: argument #1 = a argument #2 = b	CØNJG	C	C
Type Conversions: 1) conversion of argument to integer type	INT IFIX IDINT	R R D	I I I
2) conversion of argument to real type	REAL FLØAT SNGL	I I D	R R R
3) conversion of argument to double-precision type	DBLE	I,R,or C	D
4) conversion of argument to complex type (Note: if only one argument is given, it will become the real half of the complex value, and the imaginary half will be zero.)	CMPLX	I,R,or D	C
Modular arithmetic (argument #1)mod(argument #2) or argument #1 - $\text{INT}\left[\dfrac{\text{argument \#1}}{\text{argument \#2}}\right]\left[\text{arg. \#2}\right]$	MØD AMØD DMØD	I R D	I R D
Double-precision product (argument #1)(argument #2)	DPRØD	R	D

APPENDIX B
Groups of Numbers for Data Input Assignment in Programs

This appendix contains groups of numbers that may be used by a student or an instructor to designate a common (easily-defined) set of data in testing the operations defined in Fortran programs. Several variations are given in this complete data set, and each group may be distinctly referenced by its group number.

A. Integer Numbers

#1	#2	#3	#4	#5	#6	#7	#8	#9	#10
14	18	72	44	26	36	31	22	21	70
53	56	17	29	28	34	20	6	63	64
24	84	93	98	15	57	26	41	58	94
81	62	81	13	61	32	8	6	18	51
70	5	92	4	50	60	85	67	16	88
					15	53	20	1	30
					48	65	52	12	21
					60	85	30	84	17
					12	64	0	85	10
					17	46	14	29	32

#11	#12	#13	#14	#15
99	61	75	78	6
19	15	5	90	72
19	64	92	74	91
74	7	35	89	14
6	86	25	90	36
81	91	99	40	69
21	39	96	55	40
84	63	18	64	93
44	97	36	35	61
11	1	50	58	97
85	44	90	32	12
90	10	99	44	21
27	42	58	22	54
20	5	16	18	53
74	18	54	94	97
63	91	42	15	91
44	33	12	46	58
1	30	32	48	32
17	29	56	93	27
19	28	64	39	33

B. Real Numbers

#16	#17	#18	#19	#20
11.8	51.2	76.7	59.7	46.0
93.3	94.9	27.4	68.8	3.4
65.7	72.1	37.8	4.3	0.1
80.0	81.1	89.4	86.2	8.5
56.0	88.5	78.7	98.4	51.1

#21	#22	#23	#24	#25	#26	#27	#28	#29	#30
47.9	52.1	2.7	29.0	67.4	153.53	900.98	878.82	206.35	24.86
95.8	68.1	94.1	68.2	55.5	520.91	559.78	901.20	324.88	44.59
93.6	73.0	95.5	42.2	3.1	498.87	349.82	673.40	988.27	304.51
56.1	16.1	40.8	34.1	57.8	167.49	403.53	407.44	917.48	610.82
21.9	98.0	67.6	52.6	77.6	792.14	632.27	766.25	883.18	667.47
56.5	72.3	65.0	25.7	27.0					
72.3	70.2	63.7	76.2	14.6					

					#31	#32	#33	#34	#35
76.2	63.3	20.1	42.5	60.2					
53.1	31.0	89.9	66.0	76.5	408.818	935.642	117.943	999.491	990.672
60.5	31.9	64.8	21.2	72.2	629.819	624.763	917.773	845.496	980.073
97.7	79.1	56.9	82.0	25.5	115.351	919.194	797.561	824.781	974.299
26.6	82.5	22.4	25.6	64.6	491.167	839.964	876.552	605.812	339.319
74.3	79.2	94.2	11.6	62.0	405.839	86.264	888.886	362.642	662.253
37.5	40.5	49.9	76.5	12.6	631.350	64.664	577.129	720.827	526.707
33.1	68.8	88.1	63.8	64.1	773.202	669.264	958.301	475.464	492.383

C. Double Precision Numbers

#36	#37
1.63892477669	65.83138857504
34.47617032875	14.88324413597
23.21953416949	61.64234072812
67.24568350829	10.59204542764
58.74525774229	91.13221999595

D. Complex Numbers

#38	#39	#40
7.9 + 4.0i	15.0 - 0.59i	0.47 + 9.14i
0.4 + 7.3i	32.3 + 0.88i	0.52 - 3.90i
9.9 - 0.1i	5.3 + 0.00i	0.22 - 1.64i
4.5 + 0.2i	6.6 - 0.23i	0.44 + 1.33i

E. 15-digit Numbers (used as integer numbers; broken into subgroups; real numbers if a decimal is to be inserted; etc.)

#41	#42
767971478013300	870747966695725
866451265992259	571028042825280
989479606764760	645849609698253
457666613475470	665203469390449
715006456891402	424160784469618

Fortran Statements

Pages *205* and *206* provide a summary of FORTRAN key words, their description, and illustrating examples.

This summary might be more useful to you if it were cut out of the book. If so, do it.

FORTRAN STATEMENTS USING FORTRAN KEY WORDS

WORD	Description	Illustrating Example
(1) CALL	accesses statements in a subroutine	CALL ADD(A,B,C,N)
(2) COMMON	allows a memory location to be accessed by a program and subprogram(s) alike	COMMON X,Y
(3) COMPLEX	declares a variable name to maintain both real and imaginary values	COMPLEX E,R
(4) Computed GO TO	sends program execution to the statement number (given in parentheses) in the position indicated as the value of the accompanying integer variable	GO TO(100,15,121,76),I
(5) CONTINUE	does nothing except allow execution to proceed to the next statement	100 CONTINUE Note: The CONTINUE statement usually has an accompanying statement number
(6) DATA	places a value into a variable's memory location	DATA VALUE/3.32/
(7) DIMENSION	declares a variable name to have one or more sets of subscripts	DIMENSION ARRAY(50,25)
(8) DO	signifies the beginning of a group of statements to be executed at least once (Also, see implied DO)	DO 250 I=1,M,N
(9) DOUBLE PRECISION	declares a variable to be capable of retaining a more precise value	DOUBLE PRECISION PI,B
(10) ELSE	destination of program execution for a "not true" logical expression in a "block-IF" group	ELSE
(11) END	signifies the last statement in a program or subprogram	END
(12) END IF	the last statement in a "block-IF" group	END IF
(13) ENTRY	denotes a point of entrance to logic in a subprogram	ENTRY ADD2(I,J,D1)
(14) EQUIVALENCE	gives a memory location more than one referencing name	EQUIVALENCE(A,B)
(15) FORMAT	indicates the layout of input and output	FORMAT(1X,12F5.1)
(16) FUNCTION	the first statement in a FUNCTION subprogram	FUNCTION SUM(A,B,N)
(17) GO TO	unconditional transfer of program execution to a numbered statement	GO TO 25
(18) IF(arithmetic expression)s_1, s_2, s_3	statement number s_1, s_2, or s_3 will be executed next if the value of the arithmetic expression is negative, zero, or positive, respectively	IF(X−Y)10,20,30

WORD	Description	Illustrating Example
(19) IF(logical expression)statement	indicates the execution of the included statement if the logical expression is true; otherwise the next statement is executed	IF(X.LE.10.)GO TO 80
(20) IF(logical expression)THEN	the first statement in a "block-IF" group; if the logical expression is true, then the next statements are executed in order; if not true, then the next statement executed is after the END IF (or ELSE if in the "block-IF" group)	IF(I.NE.2)THEN
(21) IMPLICIT	allows the redefinition of the "first letter rule" for variable names	IMPLICIT REAL(A-N),INTEGER(O-Z)
(22) "Implied" DO	a DO grouping especially made for an I/O list	see "READ"
(23) INTEGER	declares variables to be of integer type	INTEGER X,TRIPS
(24) LOGICAL	declares variable to be of logical type	LOGICAL RESULT
(25) PRINT,list	free-format output of listed variables	PRINT,XYZ,ABC
(26) READ	indicates input is to be received Formatted: specifies unit to receive input, format number, and list of variables to be assigned values from the input provided (Example includes implied DO) Free-Format: allows data to be separated by delimiters on input; no format statement required	READ(5,75)A,(B(J),J=1,N) READ,A,D
(27) REAL	declares variables to be of real type	REAL MONEY,INTER,M
(28) RETURN	used in subprograms to transfer execution back to point of subprogram referencing	RETURN
(29) STOP	used to terminate execution of a program	STOP
(30) SUBROUTINE	the first statement in a SUBROUTINE subprogram	SUBROUTINE ADD(X,Y,Z,I)
(31) WRITE	indicates values are to be transferred from memory as output; specifies unit to receive output, format number, and list of variables whose values are to be output	WRITE(6,100)A,B,X

Index

Arithmetic assignment statement, 21, 41
Arithmetic operations, 19
Block-IF structure, 82-84
CALL statement, 126-127, 185
Code:
  binary, 8, 9
  macro, 8, 9
  object, 8, 59
  octal, 8, 9
Coding requirements, 55-57
Coding sheet, 55, 56
Comment card, 57
COMMON statement, 178-181
Compiler, 7, 8
COMPLEX statement, 173-175
Computer:
  arithmetic unit, 5
  controller, 2, 5
  IBM 370/158 system, 6, 7
  input, 2
  memory, 2
  output unit, 5
  program execution, 8
  terminal, 3, 4, 5
  time-sharing, 14-15
Computer organization, 5
Constant, 18
CONTINUE statement, 93
Data cards, 47
Data for problems, 201-202
DATA statement, 42
Debugging, 65-66
DIMENSION statement, 97, 187
DO loops:
  implied, 110
  nesting, 94-95
DO statement:
  general format, 92
  nesting of loops, 94-95
DOUBLE PRECISION statement, 171-173
Drum, magnetic, 2
ELSE statement, 84
END IF statement, 83
END statement, 63, 125, 126
ENTRY statement, 183-186

EQUIVALENCE statement, 181-183
Example problems:
  area by coordinate method, 100
  area of rectangular lot, 59
  average velocity of water flow, 64, 71, 75, 79, 142
  borrow pit volume calculation, 102
  determination of two legs and included angle of a triangle, 127
  linear regression line, 159
  matrix manipulations, 151-158
  plotting, 137
  reactions for simple and cantilever beams, 84-87
  roots of an equation, 146-151
Expressions:
  description, 19
  examples, 23
  grouping, 20
  hierarchy of operation, 19-20, 176
  mixed mode, 20-21
  using parentheses, 21
External function, 117, 120-125
Flowcharting:
  ANSI symbols, 12
  definition, 11
  procedure, 10-14
  reference work, 14
FORMAT statement:
  "A" entry designation, 34
  apostrophe, 40
  carriage control characters, 35
  "D" entry designation, 172
  "E" entry designation, 33
  "F" entry designation, 32, 45
  general format, 31
  "H" entry designation, 40
  "I" entry designation, 31, 45
  slash, 39
  "T" entry designation, 34
  "X" entry designation, 34
Functions:
  built-in, 23-25, 117
    full listing, 197-199
    partial listing, 25
FUNCTION statement, 121
GO TO statement (unconditional):
  examples, 71, 72, 75
  general format, 69

IF statement (arithmetic), 73
IF statement (logical):
  general format, 73
  logical operators, 74, 176, 177
  relational operators, 74, 176
IF-THEN statement, 83
IMPLICIT statement, 170-171
INTEGER statement, 170
Job control cards, 59
Logical constants, 175
Logical operators, 176
  table of usages, 177
LOGICAL statement, 175
Machine language, 7
Manning formula, 64, 71, 75, 79, 142
Numbers:
  integers, 17
  reals, 17
PRINT statement, 50
Problem-solving process, 9-10
Processor, 7
Program formulation steps, 55
READ statement:
  free-format, 49
  general form, 44
  with implied DO loop, 110-112
REAL statement, 169-170
Record, 35
Register, storage, 2
Relational operators, 176
RETURN statement, 121, 126
Source program, 58
Statement function, 117-120
STOP statement, 63
SUBROUTINE statement, 126
Subroutine subprogram, 117, 125
"Trial and error" programming, 142
Variable:
  definition, 18
  naming rules, 18
  subscripted, 96-103, 187
  with adjustable subscripts, 187
WRITE statement:
  general format, 29
  with implied DO loop, 112-113

ENGINEERING PRESS BOOKS

Civil Engineering License Review
Covers the seven categories of problems in the National Civil Engineering Exam. A detailed solution is given for each problem.

Mechanical Engineering License Review
Each chapter begins with a detailed review of the particular topic, followed by problems and detailed solutions.

Electrical Engineering License Review
Solved problems for the Electrical Engineering Examination.

Engineer-In-Training License Review. By C. Dean Newnan
The book is organized according to the 11 subjects in the National Engineering Fundamentals Exam (E.I.T.). It contains over 400 problems with detailed step-by-step solutions. Engineering Consultants.

Engineering Fundamentals: Examination Review. By Donald G. Newnan and Bruce E. Larock
Second edition, 1978. 528 pages. Wiley-Interscience. Each chapter begins with a review of important concepts, followed by multiple choice problems and step-by-step solutions.

Engineering Economic Analysis. By Donald G. Newnan
1980 469 pages. This college textbook is for a first course in engineering economy. The 18 chapters cover everything for the E.I.T., the Professional Engineer exams, and much more. There are 130 example problems throughout the text, and a complete set of compound interest tables.

Economic Analysis For The Professional Engineer Examination
1978. 75 pages. A concise presentation of economic analysis fundamentals and professional level topics to aid in preparation for the Professional Engineer examination. This is followed by problems with detailed solutions, and a set of compound interest tables.

Being Successful As An Engineer. By W. H. Roadstrum
1978. 246 pages. The book covers chapter-by-chapter the major elements in engineering practice. It will improve and speed up the learning-by-experience process that engineers go through in their work.

For a flyer describing all these books, with prices and ordering information, write to

Engineering Press, Inc.
P.O. Box 1
San Jose, California 95103